KONSEPBOOKS
ASTROLOGY . FENG SHUI . INSPIRATIONS

Hiya all,

As we enter the Horse Year, are these the questions going through your head?

Can you increase your net worth this year?
Will you find love with someone special?
Is your health going to be a problem?
Can you get a BIG break this year?

Getting this latest edition of Fortune and Feng Shui for 2014, your personalized horoscope text for the new year, will make it possible for you to not only investigate your luck, but also to show you how you can identify and dissolve the obstacles coming your way and how you can ENHANCE the good fortune that is coming.

You can study the feng shui winds and energy patterns that will influence your luck at work, in business, in your love life and for your physical well being for the coming year.

In this little book, we explain the forces influencing the luck of your animal sign and alert you to what you can expect and how you can stay protected against bad influences and expand auspicious indications in the different areas of your life.

Discover the wonderful benefits of Feng Shui that go hand in hand with astrological information that we have incorporated in this little book. Yes, there is plenty of information inside!

And also, can I invite you to join my Feng Shui "family". By subscribing to my fortnightly newsletter, I will send you updates chock full of feng shui stories, fabulous anecdotes from my past, present and future experiences investigating and doing the feng shui of many people and companies from around the world. There will also be lots of tips covering all three dimensions of feng shui - space, time and spiritual - and up-to-date news of new books, cures and enhancers. It also allows me to answer your questions that will benefit others too.

Our newsletter is FREE and it is easy to register. Just go to *www.wofs.com* and sign in!

All the best,
Lillian

Fortune & Feng Shui 2014 ROOSTER
by Lillian Too and Jennifer Too

Published by KONSEP LAGENDA SDN BHD (223 855)
Kuala Lumpur 59100 Malaysia

For more Konsep books, go to www.lillian-too.com or www.wofs.com
To report errors, please send a note to errors@konsepbooks.com
For general feedback, email feedback@konsepbooks.com

ISBN 978-967-329-124-3
Published in Malaysia, August 2013

ROOSTER

The most outstanding thing about the Rooster personality is the sense of purpose you bring to everything you do. You are a highly resourceful person for whom most things seem possible. Indeed, once you take on something, you are the type who will see things through to successful completion no matter how difficult the going gets. You rarely give up, as a result of which the Rooster gets increasingly respected as you get older. You have the potential to achieve great heights of success.

Direct and down-to-earth, the Rooster can be described as a perfectionist and this puts others off you simply because you set the bar too high. You can also be quite judgmental of others and the young Rooster is often too frank and forthright for their own good. You would have a wider circle of friends if you were less vocal about your views and opinions.

This is a good year to relax a little, not be so tense, not try to achieve too much and definitely not to expect too much from yourself or from those who work with you or for you. Younger Roosters would benefit from having a sense of humour. Do not take

yourself too seriously. Roosters are generally supremely confident and unbowed by convention. However, 2014 is a year when you might feel self-doubt creep over you. This is because you do not feel that strong this year. This can eat into your self-esteem, which is not necessarily a bad thing, because it gives your softer inner self a chance to exert itself.

This is a year when your awesome intellect and creativity will bring new admirers into your orbit so that professionally, you will easily impress a new set of like-minded people. Attaining excellence comes easy for you even when you may not be operating at your best.

You learn fast and you have the staying power to see everything and anything you start right to the end. There is always a clear purpose to your activities. This wins you the respect of many important people. The only problem is that sometimes you get so lost in what you do that you need to be reminded that there are others working with you! Open your arms to the presence of others and you will be far more effective.

ROOSTER - BORN CHART

BIRTH YEAR	WESTERN CALENDAR DATES	AGE	KUA NUMBER MALES	KUA NUMBER FEMALES
WOOD Rooster	13 Feb 1945 to 1 Feb 1946	69	1 East Group	5/8 West Group
FIRE Rooster	31 Jan 1957 to 17 Feb 1958	57	7 West Group	8 West Group
EARTH Rooster	17 Feb 1969 to 5 Feb 1970	45	4 East Group	2 West Group
METAL Rooster	5 Feb 1981 to 24 Jan 1982	33	1 East Group	5/8 West Group
WATER Rooster	23 Jan 1993 to 9 Feb 1994	21	7 West Group	8 West Group
WOOD Rooster	9 Feb 2005 to 28 Jan 2006	9	4 East Group	2 West Group

CONTENTS

PART 1.
LUCK OF THE ROOSTER IN 2014

PART 2.
HORSE YEAR 2014

PART 3.

ANALYSING YOUR LUCK IN EACH MONTH

PART 4.

FENG SHUI OF THE ROOSTER'S LOVE LIFE IN 2014

PART 5.

ROOSTER'S PERSONAL FENG SHUI IN 2014

PART ONE
LUCK OF THE ROOSTER IN 2014
General Prospects for the Year

Wood Rooster	- 69 years
Fire Rooster	- 57 years
Earth Rooster	- 45 years
Metal Rooster	- 33 years
Water Rooster	- 21 years
Wood Rooster	- 9 years

LUCK OF THE ROOSTER IN 2014

A blessed year with outstanding success luck to look forward to

Those born in the year of the Rooster will enjoy spectacular success luck in 2014. This is the most outstanding aspect of the Rooster's destiny in this year of the fiery horse. There is cause to be optimistic about all kinds of outcomes this year in spite of the conflict stars and the danger of your energy getting exhausted as the year progresses. This year you will discover the joys of reaping the benefits that come with having a powerfully strong personal *Lung Ta* or Wind Horse. This year 2014, your Wind Horse luck, which brings success, is at an excellent level!

Big SUCCESS is definitely possible this year because the Rooster's personal *lung ta* is at an excellent level.

Last year you had some acrimonious and disturbing energies to deal with, but this year the Rooster enjoys a very blessed year when there is great harmony and plenty of heavenly blessings shower down on you. Heaven luck is brought by the power of this year's Flying Star feng shui winds. This is thus a very good year to perform the ritual of releasing the lung ta into the skies. Do this as often as you wish, even as much as releasing a Wind Horse each week to enjoy a year of continuing success.

The ritual of sending the Wind Horse into the skies has been in existence amongst the mountain people of China and Tibet for centuries. It involves hoisting the Wind Horse together with its powerful mantra as high into the skies as possible. Previously, when balloons had not yet been invented, flags carrying images of the Wind Horse can be seen on roof and mountain tops. Today, while this practice continues to be practised, it has taken on religious overtones.

In fact, raising the Wind Horse is very much a spiritual practice and it brings wealth luck. It is especially effective for the **57 year old Fire Rooster** and the **33 year old Metal Rooster**, both of whom have very strong wealth-making luck this year. You are both in the prime of your life, one at an age to reap the benefits of a life of hard work, while the other is just starting out on your quest to make it big.

You and other Roosters like you can release a string of 21 flags containing the image of the Wind Horse printed on cotton cloth or lightweight paper, and

Releasing Wind Horse flags to the skies increases your success luck.

containing the Wind Horse activating mantra. Tie these images and mantras to helium-filled balloons to be released into the skies on a bright sunny day or during a cloudless night. This ritual is best done as a group, with friends or alone. Done with friends it is powerful when you all have the same motivation – i.e. to attract greater success and prosperity into your lives.

Each week, you can also release a few balloons carrying 21 flags each, to ensure that success luck materializes for you. This is a powerful ritual that activates success luck. When the Wind Horse flies into the skies, it opens up pathways to abundance for those whose personal Wind Horse is strong!

The idea is for your personal Wind Horse to fly as high as possible. For those who want to activate for wealth luck, you can attach the flag of the **White Dzambhala sitting on an Azure Dragon** with the four Offering Goddesses.

Flying the White Dzambhala is one of the most effective ways of raising your wealth luck! These wealth and success rituals work best when they can fly really high. If necessary, use three or more balloons instead of one!

The Rooster will not be feeling strong this year, and in fact you could well be feeling weak. This year you face serious challenges to your physical well being. Health is an issue and it is important to be careful with your food intake. Watch weather changes and be mindful of new strains of flu bugs and allergies. Older Roosters should be mindful of over-exerting yourselves.

The Rooster is also directly hit by the **Star of Reducing Energy** flying into your home location of West, causing you to succumb to extreme tiredness, insufficient sleep and for some of you, a good measure of mental stress. You need to work at generating extra radiance to make your aura glow. You must not allow yourself to feel disinterest towards your work or your life. This is the feeling that can well overwhelm the Rooster in 2014.

It is not a bad idea for the older Rooster-born who might be feeling jaded or fed up with life to consider going on a long vacation – a cruise or spa holiday to let your body rest and rejuvenate.

Often, this kind of letting go can be an excellent way to counter the effects of a weak life force, precisely the affliction you are suffering from this year. This together with your weakened spirit essence can make you succumb to bouts of moodiness, when feelings of insecurity can wash over you even when there really should be no cause at all to feel this way.

The energies around you make you want some really tender loving care; thus it is those amongst you who are surrounded by friends and family who tend to be happier than those of you who are living by yourselves. In other words, you need some good cheerful company to make you feel uplifted. You need some happiness energy!

And here is where there is plenty of good news for Roosters. This year, auspicious feng shui winds bring the powerful star of 6 into your home location. This is a very auspicious star number. It generates the actualization of heaven's blessings and will help you overcome feelings of depression that might occasionally overwhelm you.

The Rooster is definitely not at your best this year, so you are unlikely to be sociable. Even when you enjoy good success luck, which adds to your list of attainments, you find it hard to feel celebratory. The number 6 star however will bring some unexpected new developments, which come as a pleasant surprise. It will be something heavenly and it will surely lift your spirits.

In 2014, it is not wise to take either your physical or mental wellbeing for granted.

Physical strength nurtures the inner spirit, which in turn is what can give you the steely backbone you need to feel confident and powerful. The important thing here is to know that you cannot be operating at your peak all the time; nor will years of hard luck continue without abating.

The Rooster has had several exhausting years of rather challenging luck. You need to reinvigorate your body and mind so that weak energies get transformed – like forging steel with fire. The last year and this year are Fire years, which test the Rooster's Metal.

The financial luck of the **57 year old Fire Rooster** and the **33 year old Metal Rooster** is very strong, and you can easily benefit from heavenly star of 6 and also your strong *lung ta*. The big success luck associated with a strong Wind Horse has every chance to manifest for you.

Remember to perform the ritual to raise the Wind Horse, which we have already described to you. And for the **45 year old Earth Rooster**, add extra Fire element energy by using red balloons to activate wealth luck. The Fire element can also be symbolized by the presence of candles as you release the Wind Horse image. You can also **wear the colours red or white** to energize your personal Wind Horse.

FENG SHUI ENHANCER: Wear the Wind Horse in white gold on your body as a jewellery pendant or place the **bejeweled Wind Horse** with a wish granting jewel on its back and Wind Horse amulet on its side on your desk. These placements add extra zest to everything you do.

It is a good idea for the Rooster to lighten your workload this year. You might consider refusing to take on too many responsibilities, as this will only cause you to feel dissatisfied with yourself. Taking on too many things - especially activities that are more social than commercial - undermines your inner spirit and will distract you. They will dilute your effectiveness, because the Rooster is more a commercial sign than a charitable sign. You are simply not cut out to be a social worker! In any case, you will be swamped with self doubt every so often this year, simply because you are not as strong as you wish you to be.

This is due to the astrological influences of the year impacting on you. Do not be hard on yourself for seeming to be weak and indecisive. Refrain from taking on additional new responsibilities. Conserve your energy. In terms of health luck, the younger Roosters are more vulnerable to illness afflictions than the older Roosters. Thus older **Wood and Fire Roosters** have little to worry about in respect of their health, while the younger **Metal and Water Roosters** have more reason to worry.

The key to creating a really good year for the Rooster is to be as alert as you can when something potentially exciting creeps up on you. There are some unexpected but pleasant surprises in store, and in the year of the Horse, even a small opportunity can grow into something big.

It is better if you do not rely on your "instincts". Your own good sense and down-to-earth expectations should be enough to tell you when something good comes along.

In any case, being a Rooster, you are a practical sign, unlikely to chase after anything inconsequential or lacking in substance. This year, your judgments require careful analysis and investigation, more so than usual. When one's life force and Spiritual Essence are at low levels, one is well advised to think things through. Avoid acting on impulse and have faith in your own success potential this year.

Shown on the following spread is your luck profile brought by the elements of the year affecting your life force and spirit essence and also your health, wealth and success luck.

This chart gives a summary of how the elements of the year affect Rooster-born people, categorized according to the heavenly stem element of your year of birth. One glance at the chart and you are immediately struck by your weak readings for life force and spirit essence being balanced out by an excellent showing for your success luck. The chart indicates your Wind Horse is at peak level this year.

Your **LIFE FORCE** is an indication of your radiance and vitality. Some years you are more active than in other years, and this is always reflected in a strong life force. Vitality is an indication of how strong your mind is and it is what sustains your confidence. When your life force is weak, it needs to be strengthened. The Rooster's life force is very low, and this suggests your physical energy requires a boost. You must work at revitalizing your health. Go to the gym! Work out! And if you are older, discover the joys of taking walks in parks, but do not over exert yourself this year!

Your **SPIRIT ESSENCE** is an indicator of your inner strength. It shows how strong your inner chi essence is. Usually, when your spirit is strong, everything about you appears strong. It is harder for others to cheat you or to disturb your mind using spirit harm. Bad intentions aimed at you will naturally boomerang back. The Rooster's spirit essence is weak. This year you need to supplement your inner chi with amulets that give you good cosmic protection. Wear your **chakra amulet pendant** to strengthen your spiritual energy.

These two categories of life force and spirit essence reveal how you tend to react to difficulties, stresses and strains during the year. They reflect your inner strength and resilience; thus physically and mentally,

LUCK ELEMENTS OF THE

2014	WOOD ROOSTER 69/9 years	FIRE ROOSTER 57 years
LIFE FORCE	VERY BAD XX	VERY BAD XX
HEALTH	EXCELLENT OOO	VERY GOOD OO
WEALTH	BAD X	EXCELLENT OOO
SUCCESS WIND HORSE	EXCELLENT OOO	EXCELLENT OOO
SPIRIT ESSENCE	VERY BAD XX	VERY BAD XX

The indications of the five aspects of luck affecting the prospects for Roosters in 2014 are summarized in this table.

ROOSTER IN 2014

EARTH ROOSTER 45 years	METAL ROOSTER 33 years	WATER ROOSTER 81/21 years	YEAR ELEMENT
VERY BAD XX	VERY BAD XX	VERY BAD XX	FIRE
NEUTRAL OX	VERY BAD XX	BAD X	METAL
VERY BAD XX	VERY GOOD OO	NEUTRAL OX	WOOD
EXCELLENT OOO	EXCELLENT OOO	EXCELLENT OOO	METAL
VERY BAD XX	VERY BAD XX	VERY BAD XX	WOOD

it looks like the Rooster can be lethargic and in need of rest. The Rooster will benefit from some mental and physical revitalizing in 2014. This indication applies to every Rooster irrespective of your heavenly stem element at birth. The problem facing the Rooster is also a source of good news and this is its strong potential for success, which gives Rooster boost. So instead of resting and lying low, the Rooster will want to be very active this year.

Your Success Luck indicator which measures the strength of your personal "Wind Horse" shows an EXCELLENT reading, so your SUCCESS potential is at its peak. You can be courageous in risk-taking this year and you can be as forward thinking as you wish!

In terms of **HEALTH LUCK**, the Wood and Fire Rooster show excellent indications. But for the younger **Metal and Water Roosters**, there is cause for some concern. The latter two must strengthen their health luck by wearing **health amulets** and keeping a **Wu Lou** by your bedside. If your house faces East, you must be extra careful, as the illness star there can cause your health luck to go even lower.

The WEALTH LUCK category is an indication of your ability to attract new prosperity and for those in business. Excellent wealth luck indicates that hard work pays off bringing you a good harvest. Auspicious wealth luck indications also suggest personal power and ongoing abundance.

For 2014, the **Fire Rooster** has excellent wealth luck, while the **Metal Rooster** enjoys very good wealth luck. The two of you enjoy a comfortable year with few financial worries. In fact, income levels can see an increase and you enjoy monetary and financial stability. Unfortunately, the **Earth and Wood Roosters** do not enjoy good wealth luck in 2014. Read Part 5 of this book to fertify your wealth luck with the Dzambhala Wealth Ritual.

Overcoming the Stars of the 24 Mountains

To assess your year's luck, all the inputs that affect it should be investigated and here studying the "stars" that migrate to each of the 24 different subsectors of the compass is important. These 24 Mountains "stars" bring different influences to the luck of the twelve animal signs each year.

These stars have descriptive names and they can be positive or negative. Being aware of the quality of stars that land into or near your home location brings an extra dimension to the investigation of the fortunes affecting your sign in 2014, and to the different sectors of your home.

In this context, all three of the stars affecting the Rooster are not favourable, as the Rooster is sitting on the **Star of Reducing Energy.** This is an exhausting star. At the same time, the stars on either side of the Rooster's home location are **Yearly Conflict Stars**, which of course add to your aggravations this year.

It is highly likely that the two conflict stars will bring conflicting energy, which will distract and annoy you. Even when you consciously avoid getting into arguments with others, somehow argumentative energy will manifest for you. Nothing you see seems to be right, as those around you will find fault and seemingly pick on you. When conflict stars come near you, the best way to handle the situation is to say as little as possible. Definitely when a potential conflict situation arises, it seems advisable **not to respond at all**. Otherwise you will only feel upset and aggravated.

For the Rooster therefore, the 24 Mountains stars influencing your luck are quite negative. **Conflict energy** can manifest as jealousy, envy and harmful gossip. You must stay strong. Remember that only small-minded people pick fights and gossip with malicious intent. Most gossip is harmless if you ignore it and not give it power by paying attention. Most important is that you must not let yourself get immobilized by envious emotions sent your way. They are like poison arrows that you can disarm by thinking of the arrows as beautiful blue flowers of peace and encouragement!

It is beneficial to wear **powerful amulets** to ward off the conflict star. This amulet will ensure that you do not succumb to anxiety and nerves caused by others wanting to quarrel and find fault with you. You can still rely on your spirit essence, but it might not be strong enough to fight the effect of the Conflict Star.

FENG SHUI TIP: In 2014 it is beneficial to ensure that your own Metal energy is sustained and maintained. Thus everyone born in the year of the Rooster should definitely wear the **Tortoise Chakra Metal amulet** meant for the Rooster.

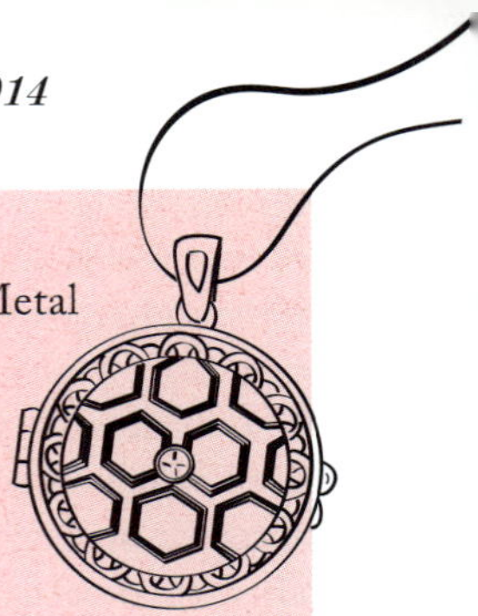

Enhancing Earth Chi with Solid Crystal Balls

Your fortunes in the year 2014 will improve if you increase the presence of Earth element energy near you. Earth element is completely missing from this year's Paht Chee chart. Place **crystal balls in five colours** to signify all five elements (this is an excellent feng shui enhancer) or place a yellow crystal ball embossed with sacred mantras of increase to magnify and expand your wealth and good fortune in 2014.

Spin the crystal ball daily on its stand to simulate the power of incantations so that everything good increases in your life. The presence of energized crystal balls is extremely effective for enhancing the fortunes of all signs this year, as they balance the year's Paht Chee chart. They are best when placed in the living area, ideally on your coffee table. The crystal balls emit powerfully strong cosmic rays that dissolve all tensions within the home.

Crystal balls help in your relationship luck with outsiders and family and improve interpersonal relationships between spouses, siblings and colleagues. Crystals are always associated with goodwill and are effective for dissipating harsh energies emitted from angry words and temper tantrums.

The Rooster is certain to benefit from the harmonizing energy of smooth crystals since your sign is afflicted by two conflict stars this year. Displaying these energized crystals will absorb the bad energy of the yearly star.

Clustering crystal balls can strengthen the luck of the Rooster as well as make up for the missing Earth energy in the year's chart.

PART TWO
HORSE YEAR 2014

A Year when Going with the Flow is Best

LUCK OF THE WOOD HORSE YEAR 2014

When Fire Energy Is At Its Height

The year of the Wood Horse is the second of the three "Fire" years that began last year. These are years when Fire energy is at its height, thrusting those born in the years of the Horse and Snake (both Fire signs) aggressively into the limelight. The more determined amongst you are those who will enjoy the greatest measure of success!

Fire energy at its height however can be fleeting.

Fire is an element that rises fast and furious but it is easily spent. This describes the extended energy of the year and it is easy to imagine a powerful horse galloping strongly. It will be risk takers who make it or break it who will stand out this year.

For Metal signs such as the Rooster, Fire years can be exhausting as **Fire causes Metal signs to get burned** out. You get tired easily this year unless you are a Rooster born in the winter months, in which case the warmth of Fire brings comfort and new energy; it also brings you a new kind of creativity that opens up new directions for success. It can really be quite an exciting time for the Rooster and the only thing standing in your way will be your general lack of energy. Your life force is weak and it can be a hindrance that slows you down.

This year the four "Earth" signs - **Dragon, Dog, Sheep and Ox** - are at their strongest in terms of confidence levels and inner strength. The four signs enjoy maximum life force and Inner Essence enabling even those amongst them whose luck may not be at its best, to perform at their best. They can however help their allies/secret friends create an extended field of strong energy.

For the Rooster, a Metal sign, **it will be the Dragon on whom you can lean on for strength.** The Dragon is your secret friend and you can borrow some of its power chi for the year. **You can also borrow confidence and strength from the Ox** who is your astrological ally. Thus the Dragon lends you strength, and the Ox builds yourself assurance and confidence.

Earth is the element that brings maximum good fortune this year – so placing crystals and precious rocks and wearing gemstones energize good fortune. In 2014, wear raw **citrines** and **agates** set with faux or real, silver or gold, and fill **wealth jars** and vases with precious stones.

This advice applies especially well for the Rooster for whom the **Earth element symbolizes your clever mind**, which is what will help you transform everyday ideas into potential sources of wealth and business success. The Earth element also produces Metal and is thus very productive for the Rooster.

The Luck of the 12 Signs

In terms of success luck, it is the **Rooster, Snake** and **Ox** – the trinity of animal signs that collectively signify intellectual creativity - who will enjoy the greatest success luck. These are the visionaries of the Zodiac. Their presence in your home either as **siblings or members of your family** can bring a resolute purpose to your endeavours, thereby helping you. **Fire energy** (bright lights) add effectiveness to their efforts creating the promise of success, except for the Rooster who has to endure some difficult challenges before success can manifest.

The **Rabbit**, **Sheep** and **Boar** trinity will also enjoy success luck this year. These signs display powerful diplomatic skills which are so needed in this Horse Year when fierce energies rule. These signs will quietly walk away with the prize in any outright competitive situation and whatever gains you make will be mainly under the radar, unknown to many. These are the three signs whose success potential in 2014 will be actualized out of the limelight.

The year does not favour those who are overtly ambitious. Aggressively hankering after a promotion or appearing unscrupulous in your quest to succeed will bring on the ire of others.

It is more effective to come across solid and reliable than to appear arrogant or aggressive. It also does not hurt to adopt a persona of humility as arrogance does not sit well this year. There is already enough aggressive energy surrounding the year.

Thus the trinity of ambitious signs comprising the **Dragon**, **Monkey** and **Rat** must watch themselves, because for these three signs, success luck is not strong. Obstacles abound and there are troublemakers causing unseen problems. These signs will feel frustrated and aggravated and will need to strengthen the energy of their Wind Horse. For them, surrounding their personal space with Water energy helps. This is the element which will give a boost to the personal Wind Horse of these three signs.

Meanwhile, the **Horse,** together with its allies the **Tiger** and **Dog,** will find the year quite tough in terms of bringing work projects to a completion or to close deals they may be working on. Success luck is elusive for these free spirits of the Zodiac. For them, it might be better not to pursue tough assignments. It is better for them to focus energies on other dimensions of their lives, such as their love life or studies that opens up new career directions for them.

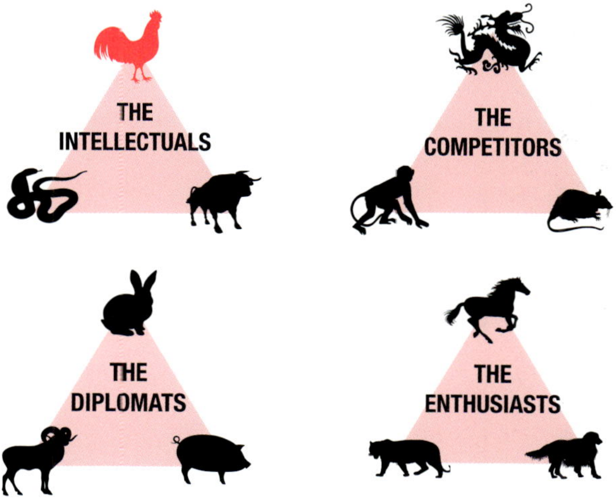

FIRE ELEMENT BRINGS WEALTH LUCK

For all signs, when it comes to wealth luck, it will be those born with the **Fire element in their heavenly stems** that will enjoy the most excellent prosperity in 2014. This includes the 18 year old Fire Rat, the 17 year old Fire Ox, the 28 year old Fire Tiger, the 27 year old Fire Rabbit, the 38 year old Fire Dragon, the 37 year old Fire Snake, the 48 year old Fire Horse, the 47 year old Fire Sheep, the 58 year old Fire Monkey, the **57 year old Rooster**, the 68 year old Fire Dog and the 67 year old Fire Boar.

For the 12 of you, the Fire element of your year heavenly stem **attracts money luck your way.** Financial stability comes easily, and for those belonging to the Earth signs, you can expect a financial windfall of some kind. It is beneficial to stay alert to what the year brings to you.

Inviting KUBERA into the Home

For everyone wanting serious wealth luck to materialize this year, it helps very much to invite **Kubera, the powerful Wealth God** into the home. Kubera is one of the eight **Lords of Horses** and brings continuing prosperity into any home that displays his image.

Kubera is the Wealth God who rules all the auspicious luck brought by Horses!

In his left hand, he holds a **yellow mongoose spouting jewels**, symbolically dropping wealth to everyone he meets up with; and in his right hand, he holds the **sword** that defeats all who would block your good fortune from actualizing. Legends say that he rides the Wind Horse, hence bringing success as well, but Kubera is mostly revered for the way he overcomes obstacles that block wealth luck from manifesting.

The image of Kubera is on the cover of this book. Simply keeping this book in your handbag or in your home symbolically brings in his auspicious image, although it is even more auspicious to get a bejeweled figurine of Kubera to place on your work desk. Some say Kubera is also revered in Tibet as the powerful **Golden Dzambhala**, who also brings wealth luck.

Luck of those Born in Winter Months

The year 2014 benefits those born in the **winter months**, because the warmth of Fire energy provides reassuring comfort, strengthening those weakened by the biting cold of their winter birth. The Chinese believe that the weather conditions that greet us when we are born have a lasting cosmic effect on our luck profile through the years.

If you were born from September through to March, and especially if you were born in January or February, the winter months, this will be a year when very good things have the potential to actualize for you.

Many of you born in winter months will likely have already experienced one good year of the Snake, because the previous year was also a Fire year. But this Year of the Horse is even more red, thus even more fiery! Indeed, red signifying the element of Fire is probably the only element where there simply cannot be too much! Thus you will see later in the section that there is very strong Fire energy in the year's Paht Chee chart and it is **all Yang Fire**.

In fact, there is so much Fire in the chart that it cannot be described as a balanced chart at all.

There is missing EARTH and missing WATER. Yet for 2014, with the WOOD element strengthening the FIRE of the Horse in a productive cycle, one can say there may well be an excess of FIRE!

Nevertheless, what is not so well known is that when there is this kind of excess indicated, then far from suppressing the Fire energy, **one should step up the presence of FIRE** element in our lives to participate in the fiery yang chi of the year. As such then, wearing red benefits everyone! Displaying red benefits, and keeping the home well lit benefits!

For those born in winter months then, wearing red and surrounding yourself with red is even more beneficial. **This is the key tip for the year.** Generate as much powerful yang Fire chi energy as you can if you wish to activate wonderfully flowing abundance luck.

MAKE USE OF THE COLOUR RED: The colour red has always been a great favourite when it comes to generating copious amounts of good fortune luck. Indeed, the Chinese always wear red when they wish to activate prosperity luck during the first fifteen days of the New Year, or during double happiness occasions. To activate the fiery year of 2014, this applies more than ever.

2014 PAHT CHEE CHART

YEAR OF THE WOOD HORSE

HOUR	DAY	MONTH	YEAR
YIN METAL	YANG FIRE	YANG FIRE	YANG WOOD
DESTRUCTIVE harms branch	STRONG yang fire	PRODUCTIVE benefits stem	PRODUCTIVE benefits branch
YIN WOOD	YANG FIRE	YANG WOOD	YANG FIRE
RABBIT	HORSE	TIGER	HORSE

The Paht Chee Chart of 2014 is skewed very much in favour of the Fire element, and in fact, there are only three elements present – there are 4 FIRE, 3 WOOD and 1 METAL. This is an unbalanced chart with EARTH and WATER missing. Normally, such an unbalanced chart would suggest a year that is lacking in good news, but note that the Year Pillar comprises Wood and Fire in a productive relationship. This suggests that the year is likely to bring beneficial energy indeed. Plus with so much Fire and with the essence of the year being strong Yang Fire, it seems that **a special luminosity shines** brightly on everyone for the next twelve months. A new sense of aggressiveness will prevail, accompanied by a certain bravado with a great show of arrogance even – two of the pervasive attributes of Horse years.

Except that in 2014, because it is a **Wood Horse**, this brings strong and rebellious chi energy. The chart shows not one but TWO horses – in the Year Pillar and Day Pillar.

Two horses like this suggests the presence of the Star of Aggressive Sword.

It is a year sorely in need of anger management; the year will see quick tempers, wrathful energy and an aggressiveness that colours most people's behaviour. Leaders take on great posturing, and internationally, the fiery energy could bring the world to the brink of war. Looked at from this perspective, it is a dangerous year indeed. We need diplomats this year. World leaders born in the years of the **Rabbit, Sheep** and **Boar** can successfully calm angry energies; definitely few of the other signs can.

In households, what can calm the fiery energy of the year is the **presence of the Dog**. Any family or household who has someone born in the year of the Dog living with them will find that the mere presence of the Dog can subdue aggravating behaviour and soothe troubled nerves.

The Dog-born plays two crucial roles in 2014; it complements the Tiger/Horse appearance, creating a powerful trinity of free spirits, but with the Dog keeping the other two of its allies down-to-earth. The Dog, being an Earth sign, also brings precious grounding energy and common sense, and in 2014, the added attribute of creative intelligence. The Dog also has strong life force and chi essence.

So, adding a Dog-born into your circle of friends is most beneficial.

You can also get yourself a puppy, a real dog so that its constant lively barking brings additional good vibes. You can also bring in the image of a dog, a painting or photograph, soft toy or porcelain decorative figurine.

The Paht Chee chart of 2014 shows that the Year and Month Pillars are defined by strong YANG FIRE – with Wood strengthening Fire. The Day Pillar is Fire stem and Fire branch – also strong Fire! Thus, it is Fire element energy that dominates three of the year's four pillars. There is a preponderance of Fire and it suggests the influence of *celebrity status,* with recognition and fame factors dominating the world's consciousness; there are also strong competitive pressures.

HIDDEN EARTH COMPENSATES

Note that Earth is missing, although fortunately, there are **two Hidden Earth** in the chart. The Earth element is the superstar this year; this element brings abundance and success through its attributes of creativity and intelligence.

Note that Earth exhausts Fire and in 2014, this is a good thing indeed, because it keeps the year's strong Fire energy under control without putting it out.

Thus while there are two missing elements in the chart (Earth and Water), it is the Earth element that will be the more favourable of the two for enhancing our feng shui and our luck. So although Water is also missing, it is less desirable as an enhancing element this year.

Why? Because Water will strengthen Wood, which in turn, will strengthen an already strong Fire. Water will also put out Fire, and this is not necessarily beneficial. Fire must be controlled! It should not be extinguished!

Thus in 2014, what we want is Yang Earth and Yin Water as enhancing as well as remedial agents. Yin Water will not harm Yang Fire, and as a remedy for feng shui afflictions this year, Yin Water cures are also very desirable.

Pillars of the 2014 Chart indicate two productive pillars, which bring strong money-making energies to the first half of the year. Wood strongly enhancing Fire! For those wanting to make quick and big money, the first half of the year is the time to do so, taking advantage of cosmic forces that are conducive to wealth accumulation. But by the third quarter, Fire energy gets out of control, and by the end the year, the source of the wealth - the resource - will have been sadly overly exploited.

Note that in the Hour Pillar, that WOOD is destroyed by METAL. All the wealth of the year (symbolized by Metal) has overexploited the resources (symbolized by Wood) of the year!

Those exposed in the equities markets should be prudent and exit the market by the end of the first half of the year.

There is only one clashing pillar in 2014 - the Hour Pillar **where Yin Metal destroys Yin Wood Rabbit.** This suggests that the end of the year will see stresses to the world order. It is a particularly destructive situation here as it indicates that the rich will aggressively exploit the resources of the world causing instability to manifest.

STARS of 2014's Paht Chee

The year's astrological stars brought by its Paht Chee do not look promising, being more afflictive than beneficial. Indeed, all the stars that are making an appearance this year are "relationship stars". We see the **Star of the Peach Blossom** brought by the Rabbit in the Hour Pillar. The strength of this star is not great and its beneficial energy is limiting.

There is also the **External Flower of Romance**, which indicates that love relationships started this year tend to be ill-fated – not necessarily leading to a happy ending. There is heartbreak in store at the end of the year for those engaging in love affairs. There are also unhappy repercussions and break-ups.

Meanwhile, the presence of two Horses creates a "**self-penalty**", which suggests a negative outcome on new meetings and new relationships.

This brings on the Stars of Aggressive Sword, not once but twice!

The presence of this star multiplied twice, giving it greater potency, indicates an intense and aggressive environment through the year. There is a flaring up of "rebelliousness" with troublemakers championing underdog issues, real or imagined, but in any case, causing social unrest and instability.

This star definitely suggests the rise of opposition leaders who will challenge the Establishment and the social order. It can also mean the emergence of "new leaders" who will gain power by fair means or foul. Not a stable scenario!

The name of this star is **Yang Ren**, which describes a sharp blade that inflicts damage. The *Star of Aggressive Sword* can bring either very good or very bad influences – but usually its connotation is negative rather than positive.

And because this star always affects the political situation, it suggests heavy-handedness in the use of political power. This is not a favourable indication. This suggests that in countries with autocratic or strong leaders, bloodshed and violence could flare up.

WEAR PROTECTION: For everyone, it is highly beneficial to wear **powerful protection** to safeguard you from other people's unreasonable behaviour. Note that when you are at the receiving end of injustice, intolerance or plain anger, things can get out of hand very easily this year, so that small molehills can quickly escalate into situations of real danger. You will feel really helpless in these kinds of situation, so here, prevention is better than cure.

The best amulet is to wear **protection against angry people stamped on gold in the form of a medallion** to help suppress the negative effect of the two aggressive sword stars. Women can wear our amulet scarves.

It is a good idea to make **special incense offerings** to the Earth Goddesses to invoke their protection through the year. This will bring a higher probability of peace prevailing within your localized environment i.e. your village, neighbourhood or district.

When Earth spirits are appeased and happy, they tend to be peaceful, ensuring your household is not harmed by the pervasive angry energy of the year. From a Tibetan astrological viewpoint, the Earth Spirits are helpful this year.

ELEMENT SYMBOLISM OF 2014

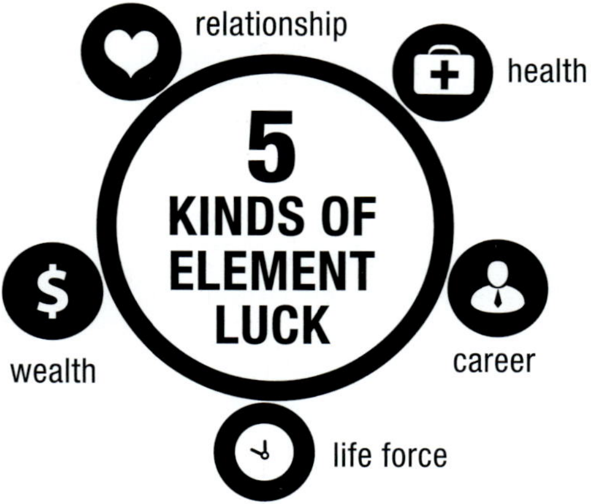

The five elements signify different types of luck each year and generally, dominant elements suggest a preponderance of the luck it symbolizes. Missing elements suggest an absence of the luck they symbolize. In 2014, there is a luck imbalance, as there are missing elements.

WEALTH LUCK in 2014 is symbolized by METAL, which appears once in the Hour Pillar. There is no hidden Metal. Wealth luck is in short supply this year. It is not an easy year to make money. It benefits those already wealthy and money is made within the context of an exploitative situation.

However, do note that those born with Fire in their heavenly stems will experience wealth luck. For others, **wearing red** and **inviting Kubera** into the home will be beneficial for attracting wealth luck.

Those of you born in the year of the Rooster, note that it is the 57 year old FIRE ROOSTER and the 33 year old METAL ROOSTER that benefit the most from wealth luck.

RESOURCE LUCK is represented by the element of WOOD. There is more than enough of this element in the year's chart with 3 direct **Yang Wood**. This supply of Wood creates strong Fire energy and ensures that **Yang Fire** burns bright and strong through the year.

The strength of Fire is both good and bad. On one hand, the Fire element is always good for recognition and fame, but Fire also manifests impulsive, impudent and aggressive energies. This can escalate into danger and because there is Wood to fuel the Fire, any negatives unleashed by Fire will be hard to put out.

2014 is an excellent year to wear gemstones such as colourful agates, citrines, amethysts, coral and turquoise, as these treasures from the ground signify powerful EARTH energy, which helps keep FIRE energy under control.

It also benefits to stay in the Earth sectors of the home i.e. in the Southwest and Northeast corners, where intrinsic Earth will help counter the strong Wood producing Fire of the year's cosmic energy pattern.

RECOGNITION LUCK also incorporates power and the attainment of high rank. This is symbolized by WATER, but in 2014, Water is missing in the main chart. But two hidden Water suggests that while direct power luck is missing, there is hidden power, i.e. the people who pull the strings are likely to stay in the background. The power brokers of 2014 are a secretive lot. The year will be awash with "conspiracy theories", especially in the last quarter of the year.

LUCK OF RELATIONSHIPS is signified by FIRE and there is so much Fire that all friendships in 2014 contain underlying tones of competitiveness. There are 4 direct Fire and one hidden Fire - many find it hard to be genuinely cooperative with colleagues and team mates.

The prevalent feeling this year is each man for himself. There are tensions at the work place. Hostile energy is prevalent and jealousy will rear its ugly head. There will be an underlying air of back biting and gossip. Politicking will make working life less pleasant.

FENG SHUI CURE: The best way to diffuse hostility brought about by competitive pressures is to place **large, heavy crystal balls** in the rooms of the home where people congregate, and in office Boardrooms. This will go a long way towards making meetings friendlier and kinder, and social occasions less tense. If you want something stronger to reduce tension and abolish politicking at the workplace, place **larger crystal balls** that have been energized by the presence of **powerful seed syllables and mantras** – in the reception area or on the Boardroom table. This goes a long way towards soothing work nerves. It subdues all hostility.

CREATIVITY & INTELLIGENCE in 2014 appears to be in short supply. It is a year dominated by emotions rather than by reason or common sense. But hidden influences bring creativity into play. The element that symbolizes creativity is EARTH, which is missing from the main chart; but there are 3 hidden Earth, one yang Earth brought by the Tiger in the Month Pillar and 2 Yin Earth brought by the Horse in the Year and Day Pillars.

For 2014, Earth is a powerfully auspicious element because it also symbolizes the luck of the Qui Ren, which indicates mentor luck. Enhancing your home or office with heavy Earth energy is thus very beneficial.

FENG SHUI ENHANCER: In feng shui, the Earth element is indicated with gemstones, natural and man-made crystals, coloured and embossed crystal balls as well as **wall plaques** decorated with auspicious and protective images. Another excellent way of introducing the Earth element is to use yellow stones. For the desk, use **eight yellow stones placed in a vase of water.** This creates the

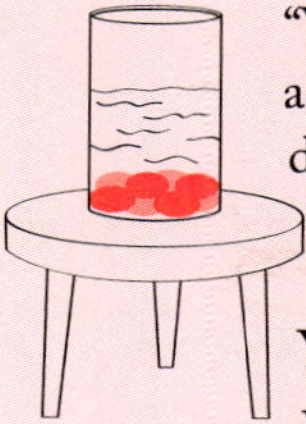

"**Yin Water & Earth**" symbol, which acts as a powerful enhancer or cure depending on where it is placed. Yin water remedies afflictions, while the stones inside the water symbolize Yin earth that brings control over the year's strong Fire energy.

The Flying Star Chart of 2014

We use the Flying Star chart of the year to analyze the pattern of energy changes that take place each year because the accuracy of the flying numbers in charting the new energies is quite stunning. We were the first to strongly emphasize the importance of studying the feng shui implications of this important chart. Today, the feng shui chart of each New Year is given great prominence by many feng shui masters around the world. This is because the chart changes each year.

At the same time, its interaction with the 24 mountain stars of the year also changes, transforming the destiny readings of each New Year. And when we also input the impact of the year's Paht Chee chart, we get each year's unique set of energies, which we can then read and summarize into these little books.

THE FLYING STAR CHART OF 2014

YEAR OF THE WOOD HORSE

	SE	SOUTH	SW	
	HEAVEN SEAL 3	TAI SUI 8	CONFLICT 1	
EAST	BIG AUSPICIOUS 2	LOVE STAR 4	CONFLICT STAR 6	WEST
	YEAR CONFLICT 7	3 KILLINGS 9	5 YELLOW 5	
	NE	NORTH	NW	

The different indicative charts point the way not only to arranging good feng shui for homes and offices through the specific placement of remedies & activators, they also offer accurate luck readings for each of the twelve animal signs.

The updating exercise is always interesting and usually very beneficial. We write our books to make it easy for everyone to improve their own feng shui and to stay connected to the new energy patterns. We also always include an entire section to monthly readings of luck in five categories of health, wealth, career, relationships and life force. This is one of the most popular sections of this book as it helps everyone stay fully updated with the good and bad stuff that comes each month. Every New Year's feng shui winds are different, in quality and in strength.

Astrological indications for the twelve signs are also not the same. Change in luck patterns can be quite drastic and it is vital to be alert to these changes. Happily, our summary of the salient points of your luck profile are all you need to stay abreast of the collective inputs of **time dimension** feng shui.

The Feng Shui chart for 2014 lays out the energy patterns that influence the attributes and characteristics of the coming Wood Horse Year. Take note of the nine sectors, each with a number representing the energy of the different sectors of any home or office, categorized according to the compass.

There is a center and there are eight sectors, each corresponding to the four cardinal and four secondary directions. Each sector is influenced by a different number from 1 to 9. These numbers symbolize different things and our interpretations rely on the strength of the different numbers, how their elements interact with the sectors, how period numbers interact with these annual numbers, and we also factor in the astrological impact of heavenly stems and animal signs.

ALWAYS USE A GOOD COMPASS

To get the most out of the analysis, you should be familiar with the different sectors of your home. You must know which corner of your home is North or South, East or West and so forth! Use a good compass to take directions from the center of the home, then mentally mark out the different compass sectors of your living and work space.

The analysis and recommendations given here will help you in your placement of cures and enhancers. You will know exactly what to do to stay safeguarded against the misfortunes of the year. Note that each level of the house or office is affected by the same chart, which can thus be used for every level. Remember that feng shui is the **Art of Placement**!

The Numbers 1 to 9

Each number has an attribute, an element and a meaning. The numbers in each sector of your house, for the current Period 8, for the year 2014 and for its own unique Flying Star chart, are different, and their interactions are analyzed in detail during extensive feng shui consultations.

For annual updates however, what you need to do is simply to suppress the afflictive stars of the year and energize the lucky auspicious stars. Hence prominence is placed on the annual number itself.

For the different months of the year we examine the **month numbers** and see how they interact with the **annual numbers.** Updating your feng shui is vital to sustaining good fortune luck. Even if you may have feng shui-ed your home exceptionally well, spent a fortune on the best Feng Shui Masters, if you do not update your feng shui according to the flying star chart of each new year, you CAN get hit by bad feng shui if your main door or bedroom or office corner is afflicted in any given year. Feng shui is a dynamic practice and the Time Dimension is a vital component of feng shui practice!

The First Step in the updating process is to identify where each of the afflictive and auspicious numbers are located in your home.

The Second Step is to know exactly what remedies to put on display to create the necessary cosmic energy to suppress the effect of afflictive numbers.

The Third Step is to energize the sectors that play host to the auspicious numbers.

While we are doing this sector by sector for all the nine sectors, please note that the effect is felt by the whole house!

The Flying Star Feng Shui Chart of 2014 is ruled by the number 4

This is the romantic WOOD star, which brings the peach blossom effect into prominence for the year. Coincidentally, this echoes the same star making an appearance in the year's Paht Chee Chart.

Those wanting to emphasize their romance luck can place all the symbols of love - **colourful mandarin ducks, lovebirds, double happiness symbols** and **lots of peonies** - in the center of your home. As these are meant for feng shui purpose, make sure you display good

quality and beautiful images, as these sublimally indicate the quality of romance luck being activated. Another excellent activator of romance luck is to place your own peach blossom animal in the center as well as in the home location of the peach blossom animal.

For those born in the years of the ROOSTER, your peach blossom animal is the **Horse**, so it is a good idea to go in search of a beautiful Horse image made either of porcelain or ceramic but preferably something bejeweled and beautiful.

You can place the horse on your coffee table in the center of the living room or in the South. This will energize romance luck that has a good chance of leading to real commitment i.e. marriage, so it should not be taken lightly. Energize this *only* if you really are interested in looking for a marriage partner!

The number 4 in the center is also excellent for strengthening scholastic luck. Because it is in the center of the chart, this can be an especially beneficial year for those wanting to gain academic achievements.

The best placement symbol is the traditional **Carp crossing the Dragon Gate**, as this is especially powerful for scholastic honours leading to your landing a super job that leads to a big career. The lowly carp is said to transform into the mighty Dragon upon successfully crossing the dragon gate. Households with school or college-going kids are sure to benefit from this auspicious placement.

THE CONCEPT OF ACTIVATING ENERGY

Note that lucky and unlucky numbers usually manifest their effects only when they get energized, so a good rule to follow is wherever sectors are afflicted by the bad numbers bringing bad luck, those sectors **should best be kept quiet**. No noisy renovations, no TV sets and definitely reduce noise levels.

In the garden, make sure there is no digging, no cutting of trees and no construction in the sectors that are afflicted. Those living in apartments also note what is taking place within view of your apartment. When there is construction work going on within view in the directions that are afflicted, use a curtain to shut out the view!

But for sectors where lucky numbers have flown to, always activate with noise with a radio or TV placed here, with bright lights, and if possible, with activity. These are the three ways to activate energy. Any of these three things will encourage yang chi to manifest to your advantage. In 2014, the three luckiest sectors are South, Southwest and West, which play host to the numbers 8, 1 and 6.

Thus if your house is sitting any of these three directions, this is a good year to undertake renovations in these sectors of your house. Doing so will activate the lucky number of the direction concerned.

Safeguarding the Northwest

Suppressing the misfortune star 5 to protect the patriarch

This year Patriarchal luck is negatively affected by the *wu wang*, i.e. the *Five Yellow*, a major misfortune star. Its location in the Northwest hits mature men who are in leadership positions. It also afflicts the luck of fathers and breadwinners. Thankfully the Northwest is a Metal sector, which exhausts the potency of 5, making it less dangerous. Unfortunately, the period 8 number of Northwest is 9, which strengthens the 5. Feng shui remedies to suppress the 5 this year must take into account these factors.

5 IN NORTHWEST BENEFITS SOME

Note that the 5 in the Northwest benefits *men* who have 5 as their Kua; basically those who are **Snake** (born 1941, 1977), **Tiger** (born 1950, 1986), **Boar** (born 1959, 1995) and **Monkey** (born 1968, 2004).

The Rooster does not feature in this group so for all Roosters, the number 5 is very dangerous. In any case the wu wang should never be activated in any way. It must be suppressed.

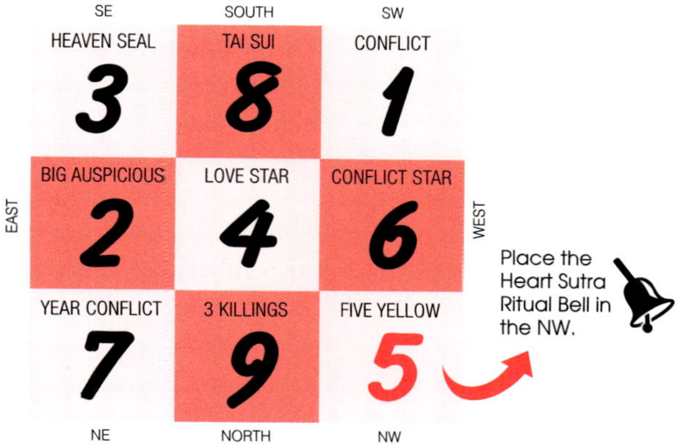

The *wu wang* is an Earth number, and since Earth is so auspicious in 2014, there is a danger that the placements of Earth enhancers might inadvertently strengthen the 5 when placed in the Northwest. So be very careful.

BE CAREFUL IN JUNE!

It is advisable to be extra careful when the monthly number 5 travels to the Northwest as that is when the 5's affliction strength gets doubled. This happens in the month of June, which is also the height of summer when Fire energy is strong, causing the 5 to be stronger.

June is thus a dangerous month for the fathers of the world and for male leaders. You will need a **strong remedy** to be put in place to protect the luck of the Patriarch in June. Misfortunes that affect the father – either an illness (which if it occurs will likely affect the lungs and respiratory system), an accident or a sudden loss of income affects the entire household.

If your house faces or sits Northwest, you definitely need to be extra careful. Bedrooms located in the Northwest can cause elderly occupants to suffer from a stroke or heart attack. It might not be a bad idea to change bedrooms for the year, thereby avoiding the 5.

REMEDIES FOR THE 5 IN THE NW:

1 The most powerful cure is a spiritual feng shui remedy. Place the **Heart Sutra ritual bell** made of brass in the Northwest of your home. The bell is designed to create the sound of metal on metal and this is a powerful way to keep the 5 subdued. This is also a powerful cosmic spiritual enhancer that gets local spirit landlords on your side, helping household residents overcome obstacles caused by bureaucratic delays and issues.

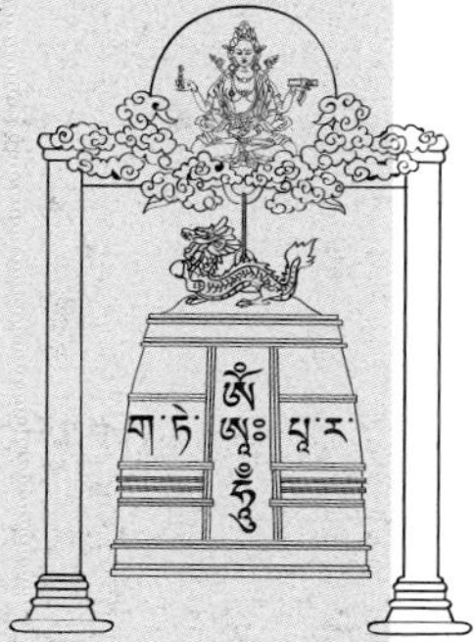

2 Another popular cure these days is to place a **music box** containing an auspicious symbol to subdue the 5. The sound of the music is metallic, and it is very popular with the feng shui masters of Hong Kong and Taiwan who swear by it. So we decided to create a music box to symbolize metal with the **Kalachakra Stupa**. Placed in the Northwest, this cure should not only suppress the 5, but also activate the Metal energy of the sector. Plus the Kalachakra Stupa always brings prosperity luck.

3 The third remedy for the 5 star in the NW is to have strong metal energy made by the tinkling sounds of the **Jade Emperor holding a windchime**. This suppresses the 5 but also invokes the patronage of the God of Heaven activating the mentor luck of this corner. This is a wonderful remedy, as it also energizes the luck of the Heavenly Mentor, who brings good fortune.

Suppressing the Illness Star 2 in the East

Protecting the eldest son against severe illness afflictions

The number 2 illness star is in the East, where it meets the Period number of 6. This reduces the severity of the illness star. Nevertheless, bedrooms or doors located here are affected by illness energy. It is advisable to keep this part of your house quiet. Excessive activity here will cause problems relating to the health of residents. The effect on the **eldest (or only) son** will be the strongest. Bright lights are not advisable. The illness star is an Earth element star, and Fire energy strengthens it.

Getting sick is unpleasant and unfortunately for the **Rooster** whose life force is low, should the illness star hit you because your bedroom or home office happens to be in the East, it can cause you a great deal of discomfort and aggravation; you need to be very aware of this and put correct remedies to subdue the illness star should it be hitting you in a room that you use frequently.

Be extra careful during the months of July and October. These are the months when the number 2 or 5 enters into your home location of West.

Hang Wu Lou windchimes to suppress the illness star.

	SE	SOUTH	SW	
	HEAVEN SEAL 3	TAI SUI 8	CONFLICT 1	
EAST	BIG AUSPICIOUS 2	LOVE STAR 4	CONFLICT STAR 6	WEST
	YEAR CONFLICT 7	3 KILLINGS 9	FIVE YELLOW 5	
	NE	NORTH	NW	

Generally, it is a good idea to keep the illness number well subdued in the East where it has flown to this year, but during July and October, the Rooster should also place the cures in your home sector of West.

CURES FOR THE ILLNESS STAR:
For the illness star affliction, we are suggesting three special remedies. If you have an important room in the East, you should subdue the illness star and you can choose the Taoist or Buddhist remedy. There is no harm in placing both types of remedies as one is a worldly cure and the other is a cosmic spiritual cure.

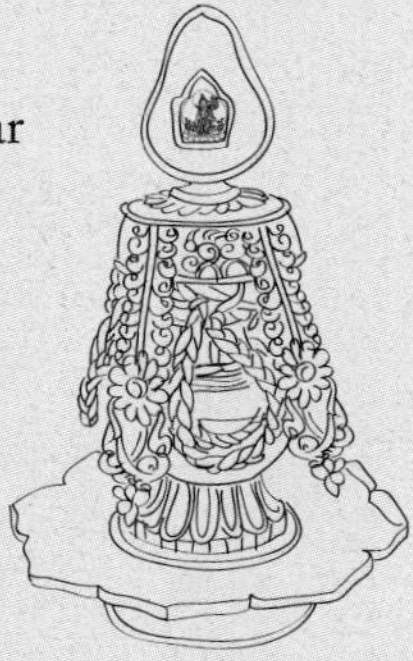

1 The Longevity Vase, this year with the image of **White Tara.** We recommend the same longevity vase as in the previous year, which featured the image of the Buddha Amityus. This year, we suggest **White Tara**, who confers wellness and longevity. The Tibetans have a great tradition for maintaining the continued good health for the older generation and also for their revered high lamas. This Vase has a special design, and is made of silver or gold and consecrated with long life mantras.

2 We have also received incredible feedback from readers and customers on how quick-acting the **Medicine Buddha** images and cures have been. Our watches and plaques have been incredibly beneficial for so many hundreds who have written in to us. This year, we have created special Medicine Buddha images with powerful mantras and made them as **fridge magnets** so that you can place them at the top of your refrigerator doors. Here, Medicine Buddha will bless all the food kept within to ensure good health for the whole household.

You can also get the **Medicine Buddha plaque,** which contains the names of all the 8 Medicine Buddhas (referred to as the 8 Sugatas) together with the powerful healing mantra. Display this plaque on the East wall in 2014 to keep the illness star subdued.

3 Note also that all the metallic remedies suggested for the *wu wang* such as the **Golden Wu Lou with Crane and Bamboo windchimes** or the **Wu Lou Windchimes** are also excellent for suppressing the illness star. Remember that the sound of metal on metal always suppresses both the *wu wang* and the illness star. This is the Taoist remedy.

Cure for the Dangerous 7 in the Northeast

Protecting the household against burglary & robbery

	SE	SOUTH	SW	
	HEAVEN SEAL 3	TAI SUI 8	CONFLICT 1	
EAST	BIG AUSPICIOUS 2	LOVE STAR 4	CONFLICT STAR 6	WEST
	YEAR CONFLICT 7	3 KILLINGS 9	FIVE YELLOW 5	
	NE	NORTH	NW	

Place the anti-burglary plaque here.

These days, home security has become a serious issue and it is really vital to stay safeguarded against the **Star of the Broken Soldier** i.e. the number 7! This is a Metal star; it is red in colour, so 7 is equated with blood, indicating armed robbery and violence. The 7 is getting more and more dangerous each year! In 2014, it flies to the Northeast, an Earth sector. This strengthens it, therefore strong remedies are needed. The 7 star manifests robbery, rebellion and violence. It is bad news in the current period of 8 as it attracts people with bad intentions into the direction it dominates, which is Northeast in 2014. If your main door faces NE, your home is afflicted by the 7. Similarly if your bedroom is situated in the NE, the 7 can hurt you. This star needs to be subdued.

CURES FOR THE NUMBER 7: For the violent star 7, very strong cures are necessary this year. For this affliction, please **do not recycle your cures,** as fresh energy works best and most effectively. We offer three special antidotes:

1 The 7 star can always be subdued with Water and especially Rhino and Elephant **Yin Water** remedy. This is because Water exhausts the Metal of 7. This special remedy calls for a set of little vases, decorated with Elephants and Rhinos, filled with water and then with **natural black river stones**. This is an important traditional Taoist cure which has been used with great success in safeguarding homes against people with bad intentions.

2 The very popular **Anti-Burglary Plaque** which contains the Tibetan Buddhist anti-burglary amulet. This has been an effective deterrent used very successfully for several years now. We have received feedback that even when petty robbers came into the house compound, they were somehow scared away before even entering the house and the only evidence of the robbers the next morning had been the discovery of a bag full of knives and *parangs* in the garden. The lady who had this experience told us her maid had woken up at 5 a.m. to go to the bathroom, and she suspects that the turning on of lights in the house must have caused the burglars to abandon the robbery.

3 For smaller homes and for apartments, you can use the **5 Element Yin Water** cure, which come in **sets of 5 to signify the 5 elements**. Placed on a sideboard or table in the NE part of the house, it protects against being cheated or robbed.

Subduing the Aggravating 3 in the Southeast

Protecting your business and job against third party bullying & hostility

The number 3 star especially when it flies to a Wood

sector, as it did last year (it was in the East last year) and is doing this year - is fierce and can be very aggravating indeed. It strikes suddenly, causing a great deal of anxiety.

Its location in the **Southeast** hits the **older daughters** of the family, especially those holding senior and influential positions. The period 8 number of the Southeast is 7, which is a violent star usually associated with burglary and other unsavoury meeting up with bad people, but the 7 here combines with the number 3 star to create a *sum-of-ten* effect. This lucky combination brings the *energy of completion*.

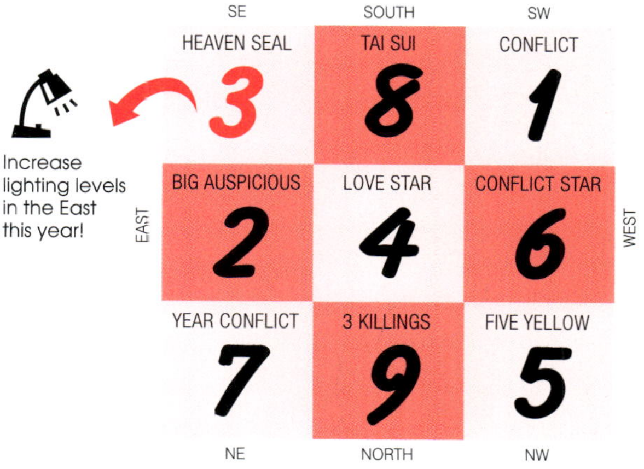

Nevertheless, it is important to suppress the number 3 star of hostility, as the aggravations that result from this affliction can escalate very fast. You must be alert to things suddenly going wrong and to anything occurring which might have been caused by this star.

You must remember that whatever manifests can easily turn into mind-blowing legal entanglements for you. Thus instead of getting angry and being too hasty in taking legal action, you are better off working at immediately strengthening your feng shui cure against this affliction.

CURES FOR THE #3

Note that the best antidote against the number 3 star is to generate the presence of FIRE energy. This can be anything at all that is painted red – a wall, a door, or a red carpet or red curtains; even nine red stones can be an effective cure. If your office is located in the Southeast, you can simply paint the walls a bright red!

As we are especially allergic to the number 3 star this year we have designed three very powerful remedies to truly suppress the 3 star in the Southeast. These are the following:

1 Framed against a red background, we have made **Nine Amulets**, each meant to dissolve the bullying and quarrelling energy of others. We have included some very strong talismans of protection including some "Tiger energy" talismans which will instantly dissolve any hostile chi sent your way. This will keep the 3 star under effective control.

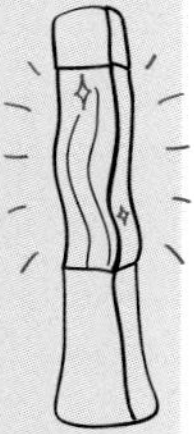

2 We are also bringing back the **Red and Gold Glitter Lamp** which we used in the previous cycle with so much success.

3 Finally, we are creating a powerful **HUM light** in red. Displayed in the home, this should completely dissolve all hostility energy that inadvertently enters. This is a cosmic remedy that radiates invisible laser-like beams of powerful pacifying energy.

Three Killings in the North

Overcoming three poisonous & harmful winds

In 2014, the North suffers from the poisonous winds of the Three Killings which is *multiplied in strength* because the 9 star is also present. It afflicts all homes facing North and brings the potential of three kinds of losses – loss of wealth, loss of good name and loss of a loved one. It should not be "disturbed" and we recommend against undertaking any kind of renovations in the North part of your home or office.

For 2014, in addition to displaying the image of **Ksitigharba and the Three Celestial Guardians** we also recommend placing the **Five Element Yin Water Cure** in the North. These are specially made small glasses printed with the five element colours. Glass is used, as this signifies the auspicious Earth energy which is so beneficial for 2014, and the five colours stones placed inside to represent the 5 element remedy.

Water is poured into the glasses to symbolize Yin Water, and five coloured stones are added inside - stones in red (fire), black (water), green (wood), white (metal) and yellow (earth). This cure is especially suitable for safeguarding the feng shui of your work desk and office. Place it on a table or sideboard in the North corner of your office. Not only will it help weaken the Three Killings it will also attract success luck into your work area!

Place it on a side board or table in the North corner of your office. Not only will it subdue the Three Killings causing it to be harmless, but will also attract success luck into your work area.

Activating 9 in the North

Creating Yang Chi with happiness events

While the North sector is afflicted by the Three Killings, it is however playing host to the auspicious and joyous number 9 star in 2014. The 9 star is a *magnifying star* but it is also regarded as the Star of

"*hei see*" which means **joyous events** such as weddings, birthdays and other happiness occasions.

If you have a door in the North, or your home is sitting or facing North, then organizing a joyous occasion in the house – a party or celebration of some kind – will be most auspicious.

9 is also the Star of Future Prosperity. So it can be regarded as a very lucky star number benefiting all homes that have a North-located main door.

What is also very encouraging for such homes is that the 9 interacts auspiciously with the sector's period number of 4 to create the Ho Tu of 4/9, which creates **Fire** energy – all this indicates that households with main doors facing or located in the **North** are likely to enjoy happiness occasions or *hei see*.

Weddings seem likely as the year is ruled by the **Peach Blossom Star**. Even the year's Paht Chee chart has the *Peach Blossom Star!* You can easily create Yang chi by throwing a party and creating noise levels. Installing bright lights will also do it – but enhancing North this way will surely be very beneficial.

Finally, the North can benefit by placing an image of the **Inukshuk** here. This is regarded by the Arctic countries as a very powerful image of mankind. It attracts success and points the way to abundance and good fortune. To be really effective for 2014, it should ideally be made up of nine stones piled into the image of man – with two limbs and two legs, although it can be made with fewer stones. As long as it resembles a standing man, it points to new success and good fortune.

The Inukshuk stone sculpture is popular in Canada and other Arctic countries, as it symbolizes all that is lucky for the **North direction.** Place this on your fish pond if you have one in your North sector. Let it channel the luck of the Arctic, "cool" down your homes – especially good for those of you born in summer months!

Energizing 6 in the West

Creating Yang Chi with happiness events

In 2014, the number 6 flies to the West sector, bringing **courage and confidence** to those born in **Rooster years** as well as to **households facing West.**

This Big Metal number flying into a Metal sector brings big benefits to the young women of the family, and especially to those wanting love and good relationships

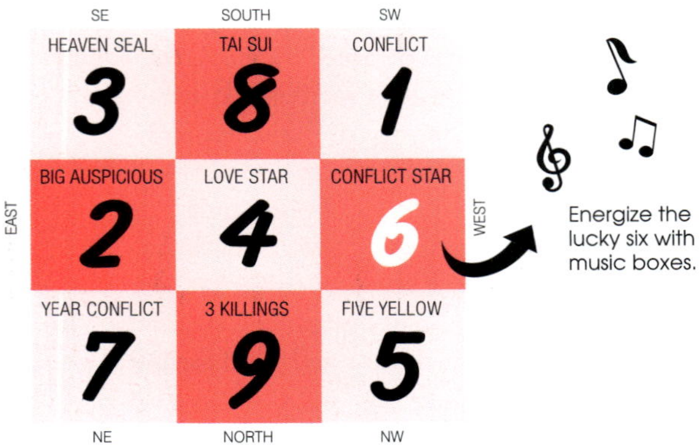

luck. The 6 here in the West favours romance and can manifest joyous events such as **weddings and engagements** for the eligible young ladies of the home. For this luck to manifest, activate with **metallic windchimes** suitably embellished with auspicious love symbols. Movement of the chimes activates the symbols, which resonate with the 6 in this sector to bring the good fortune desired.

FENG SHUI ACTIVATOR: The best way to activate the energies of the West is to have something here to get the energy moving. It is movement that causes powerful yang chi and this brings good fortune. An excellent energizer for this sector in 2014 will be the **happiness events**

musical boxes, such as with a baby in a crib or with a wedding couple! You can also display the **Jade Emperor holding a sun and moon windchime**. This would activate the power of 6 and activate the chi of the powerful sun and moon.

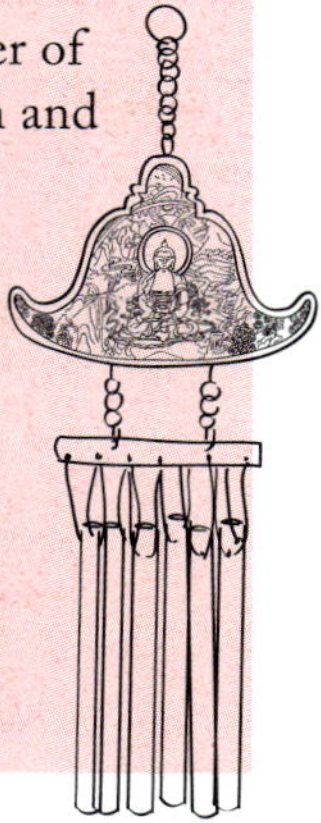

For those who would like to energize spiritual blessings of the Buddha of the Western paradise, which is Buddha Amitabha, it would be incredible to hang a **six rod windchime embossed with the celestial image of Amitabha Buddha** residing in his pure land.

Energizing 8 in the South

Creating Wealth Luck with Earth & Water

The wealth-bringing number 8 star flies to the South in 2014. This is an Earth star moving into a Fire sector, so it gets strengthened and it directly benefits the year of the Horse and houses with a South-facing exterior.

This is a strong number 8 made even stronger by the year's strong Fire energy.

	SE	SOUTH	SW	
	HEAVEN SEAL 3	TAI SUI 8	CONFLICT 1	
EAST	BIG AUSPICIOUS 2	LOVE STAR 4	CONFLICT STAR 6	WEST
	YEAR CONFLICT 7	3 KILLINGS 9	FIVE YELLOW 5	
	NE	NORTH	NW	

It also combines with the Period number 3 to create the very auspicous Ho Tu combination – one that brings excellent growth chi. It would be excellent to energize the 8 and its Ho Tu combination simultaneously. The 8 star benefits those whose bedrooms or whose homes have main doors located in their South.

Those occupying a room in this sector should hang a **large 8-rod windchime** containing the symbols of the wu lou, ingots, coins and other symbols of abundance. The windchime will create plenty of suitable metal music to attract abundance to the home.

THE EIGHT IMMORTALS MOUNTAIN

The best way to enhance prosperity luck for the whole house is to energize the 8 with the presence of a suitable mountain placed in the **South**. The presence of a mountain not only makes up for the missing Earth in the year's Paht Chee Chart but also causes **wealth luck formation** to take place. We recommend placing **Eight Immortals seated on an auspicious mountain of gold**.

This is a powerful Taoist enhancing decorative feature, which we unearthed in one of the lineage texts. The 8 Immortals sitting on a mountain signifies the Immortals in Heaven casting benevolent eyes on your home and bringing eight kinds of good fortune including wealth luck to the residents. This enhancer can be a 3D image or it can be a painting, but it should show the Immortals sitting on the mountain.

THE VAIROCANA STUPA WHICH BRINGS PEACE & ABUNDANCE

It is also extremely auspicious to place the **Vairocana Stupa** here in the South. This Stupa is embellished with the 8 Auspicious Symbols. The presence of Vairocana in the home will ensure that you are not affected by the aggressive energies of the year. This is a year when the overall energies of the world can be unstable and dangerous.

This stupa is a **peace stupa** and Buddha Vairocana protects against sudden reversals of fortune caused by natural and manmade disasters. Bringing this peace stupa, which is such a powerful holy object, into the home will activate the powerful 8 star and ensure peace and harmony in your household.

Energizing 1 in the Southwest

Creating triumphant outcomes with water

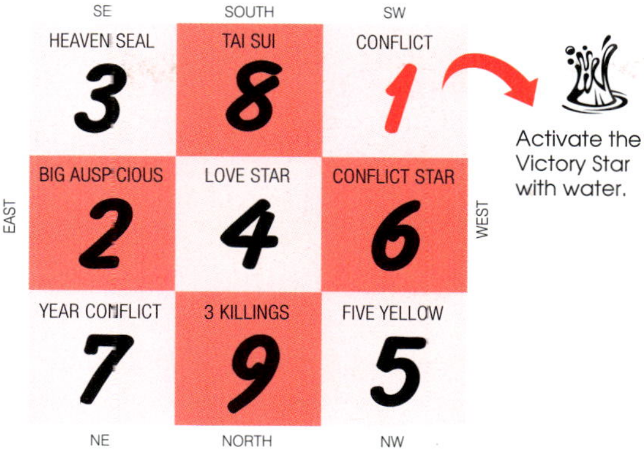

The Southwest, the place of the matriarch is blessed by the **Victory Star 1** in 2014. This star brings good fortune and quick success luck to all homes facing Southwest. If your bedroom or main door is located in this sector, you will also benefit from this auspicious white number. The best way to energize 1 in the Southwest is with **Yang Water**.

Note that in the current period of 8, water in the Southwest energizes the *indirect spirit* of the period, which brings great wealth luck. The year 2014, when the number 1 whose element is Water is here, is thus a great time to create water here (if you have not already done so!) You can create a BIG enhancer here by building a pond or swimming pool if you happen to be building your new house this year.

Creating water in the Southwest is a big wealth-enhancing tip, and for those who do not yet have water here, this is a good time to install a water feature here. This benefits the whole house.

Also note that the period number of the Southwest is 5 and water here creates the "**five ghosts bringing gold**" feature! This is a little known feng shui feature, which transforms whatever bad luck caused by gossip and politicking against you into prosperity luck. This year 2014 is thus a great time to install this feature.

VICTORIOUS GENERALS ON HORSEBACK

Lady General Hua Mu Lan benefits the matriarch

The Chinese are extremely proud of their famous generals shown riding their triumphant steeds to victory. They carry victory flags and they symbolize the luck of winning. We went to great lengths to have beautiful images of them made so they can be displayed inside homes in the Year of the Horse, actively energizing all the good qualities of the powerful general.

General Hua Mu Lan placed in the SW of the home brings luck to career women living in the house.

If you want great & lasting success that is also meaningful long term, if you are managing a large company or if you are in politics, the presence of at least one powerful general (placed in the Southwest sector) would be extremely auspicious.

And if you are a working woman with fierce ambitions to make it to the top of your profession, you can also invite in the most famous lady general of Chinese history into your home. Placed in the Southwest of the home, **General Hua Mu Lan** creates the energy of courage, confidence and victory. Men can display the image of **General Cao Cao**.

The 24 Mountains Stars of 2014

We investigate the compass stars of the 24 Mountains to add depth to the analysis of the year's sectors and for the twelve animal signs. The stars that occupy each of the 24 subdirections change every year; their influences on the luck profile of the twelve animal signs likewise change as well and for 2014, one can see at a glance that there are a lot less auspicious stars and a lot more conflict and killing stars.

THE 24 MOUNTAIN STARS OF 2014

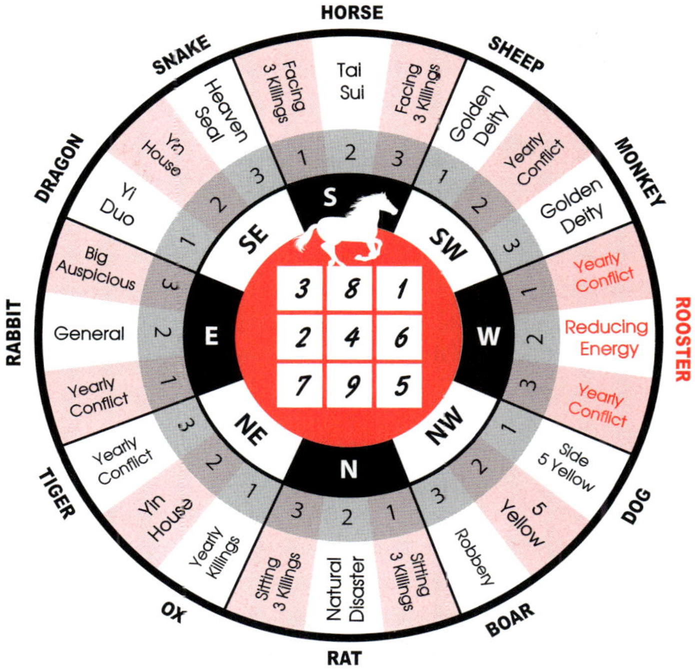

The Rooster has to contend with the Star of Reducing Energy this year. This is exacerbated by two Yearly Conflicts Stars flanking its location.

This seems to confirm the indications of the year's Paht Chee, which has already shown that there are fierce & aggressive chi energies at work, and that the Wood Horse will not be a quiet or peaceful year. Conflict energy abounds!

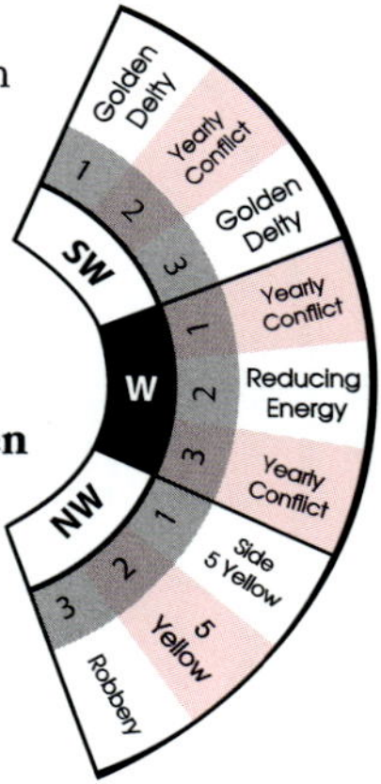

The SOUTHWEST sector benefits from the presence of the **Golden Deity stars,** so placing altars in the Southwest will be very beneficial indeed, although the heart of the Southwest is pierced by the **Yearly Conflict Star**! The image of the **Golden Chundi Goddess** and **the Golden White Umbrella Goddess Mirror** placed here will adequately subdue this Yearly Conflict Star, as well as activate the two Golden Deity Stars.

The WEST is harmed by conflict stars as well as the **Star of Reducing Energy**. The placement of **red coloured crystal enhancers** will be the most beneficial for this part of the home or office, as it would also help to quell conflit energy brought by the two Yearly Conflict Stars. This is particularly important for safeguarding the well-being of the Rooster this year.

Wrathful image of Guru Rinpoche standing on the lotus.

The NORTHWEST is hit by the **Robbery Star** and the **Five Yellow**. This is a sector that affects the man of the house and cures must definitely be put into place. Definitely the Stupa has to be placed here and also the **standing wrathful image of Guru Rinpoche** should be placed here. Guru Rinpoche is also known as the Lotus Buddha and is highly-revered as the Buddha that overcomes all obstacles and all spirit harm. Feng shui in 2014 must focus on protecting the luck of the Patriarch and nothing works better than this incredible image of the powerful demon slayer of Tibet who is revered as the all compassionate Lotus Buddha. A standing Guru Rinpoche is very rare. Make sure you invite one into the Northwest of your home to safeguard the luck of the Patriarch.

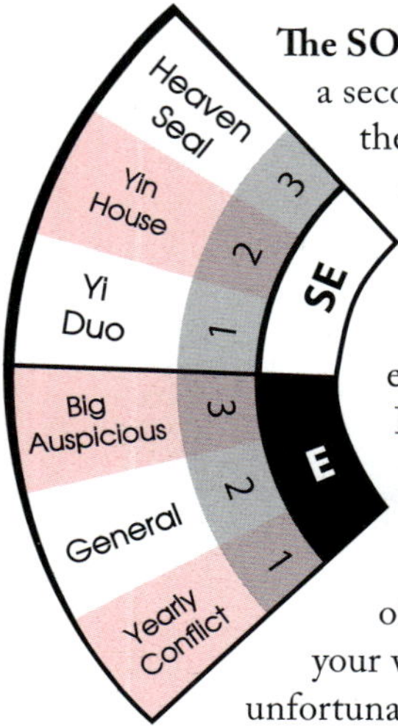

The SOUTHEAST sector is afflicted by a second **Yin House Star** but luckily there is also the calming influence of the **Heavenly Seal**. Activate this benevolent star to dispel the impact of the Yin House Star (which brings serious illness or even death to a family member). It also benefits if you can display the **Wishfulfilling Tree** of 2014 in this sector of the home. This powerful tree brings the power of the heavenly seal to actualize your wishes, while overcoming the unfortunate effects of the hostile 3 with its bright red fruit. Its growth chi directly counters the effect of the Yin House Star.

The EAST sector enjoys the single **General Star** and the **Big Auspicious Star** of the year. So for the East, display the image of a victorious general like **General Chao Chao** or **General Hua Mu Lan** to activate the General Star. To benefit from the Big Auspicious Star, place the **Wish Fulfilling Tree** in here.

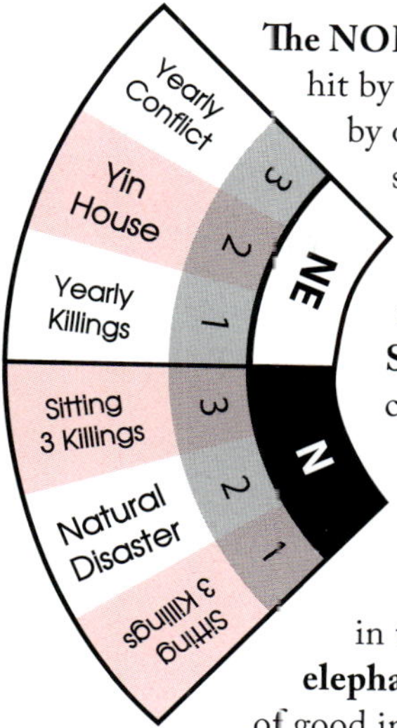

The NORTHEAST sector meanwhile is hit by the **Yin House Star** that is flanked by one conflict star and one killing star. The Northeast sector also has the violent 7 star, which brings violence. This is the sector that also houses the **Star of the Broken Soldier,** so do take note that the cure required for this sector is the **5 Element Yin Water Cure** and it is to be placed in the sector of both the Tiger and Ox, especially if you have these two signs living in the house. Place also a **pair of elephants** here to bring the weight of good intentions. This can counter the hostility chi in this sector.

The NORTH sector is harmed by the **Three Killings** and the **Natural Disaster Star**. These stars always stick together and they can create havoc. This sector also directly confronts the Tai Sui, which brings misfortune luck as well. The best cure here is to place the **Tai Sui appeasement plaques** to generate support from the Tai Sui, the God of the Year.

APPEASING THE TAI SUI

Getting the support of Tai Sui is important

Because this is such an aggressive year with conflict vibrations causing multiple pools of hostile energy in so many sectors of the compass, it is vital to keep the God of the Year appeased. The Tai Sui of 2014 sits in the location of the Horse, **in the South,** which happily houses the lucky 8 star. But note that in spite of the presence of the 8 star, it is not advisable to have any kind of renovations in the South or in houses that sit South, as this creates too much noise and will disturb the Tai Sui. It is thus better to postpone whatever plans you may have to renovate the South part of the house. Also do not cut down trees or dig big holes in the South, as this likewise disturb the peace and calm that the Tai Sui prefers. Incurring the wrath of Tai Sui will cause residents to get sick. Meanwhile the direction which conflicts the Tai Sui is North. Do not start any renovation works here. Refrain from making too much noise here and try not to sit facing the Tai Sui in the South. The best cure for the Tai Sui is to place a **pair of Pi Yao**, which in 2014 should be placed in the North and South.

PART THREE

ANALYSING YOUR LUCK IN EACH MONTH

You can enjoy fabulous success luck this year but mental stress & lack of motivation may be an issue

The Rooster has many things to look forward to this year. The feng shui chart brings the Star of Heaven into your sector, creating new opportunities to excel and opening up new directions for you to pursue. It can be an exhilarating time indeed if you can work up the motivation. Your main problem this year will be low energy levels leading to a lack of drive. The Star of Reducing Energy together with the Conflict Stars from the 24 Mountains may cause you to consider throwing in the towel when things get tough. But obstacles that arise are temporary. Do not let transient complications steer you off course. There is a lot that can be achieved this year because you have good fortune luck on your side.

FIRST MONTH
February 4th - March 5th 2014

YEAR STARTS OFF WELL WITH THE VICTORY STAR

The white star 1 makes an appearance, making a very positive impact on your life. It combines auspiciously with the number 6 heaven star, forming the *Ho Tu* of 1/6. This doubles the effects of this *Ho Tu*, which already resides in your sector from the combination formed between the annual and period star. This makes this a truly opportune time for the Rooster. You benefit from great wisdom, which allows you to make good decisions. The month favours expanding your knowledge and developing yourself further. While the energies are especially helpful to the young Rooster, they also benefit the adult Rooster. You are never too old to learn new skills, and this month could see venturing down an exciting new path.

WORK & CAREER - Fresh New Opportunities

Even in a job that has become overly familiar, this month sees you finding fresh new opportunities to transform what you do into something truly exciting with lots of potential. You feel energized by your work and successes follow on quickly from such enthusiasm.

Some of you may be made job offers that are hard to refuse, but before you make any life-changing decisions, consider your options carefully. Once you make up your mind, give it your whole heart and chances are good that things will work out wonderfully for you. Whatever your work situation, you are popular and well-liked by your colleagues and co-workers, making working life very pleasant indeed.

BUSINESS - New Initiatives

There are multiple avenues for growth, and this is the time to decide on a few of these to pursue. New start-ups, diversification and expansion may occupy you at this time. Remember that this is a month when new initiatives not only suggest themselves, but will enthuse and motivate you. Getting really involved with the business will stimulate your mind and bring new purpose to your life. Do not hold back on taking calculated risks. You have good fortune on your side which will ensure you don't get yourself burnt in the process. However, in your enthusiasm, do not put all your eggs in one basket.

LOVE & RELATIONSHIPS - Great Happiness

The month ahead is a promising one for Roosters looking for love. Even if your attentions are not focused on romance, the heavenly energies in your chart bring some very special people into your life, and perhaps one in particular. You can let go of some of your guardedness and inhibitions. When you open up and let others in, you discover a new level of happiness you were unfamiliar with before. No matter your life experiences up till this point, this month changes some of your previously firmly-held beliefs, enabling you to access a different kind of contentment.

The married Rooster has the same potential to experience some totally new kinds of joy; whether this comes from a new baby, a new home, or even just a new hobby you take up with your spouse, it is fulfilling and brings you a lot of personal happiness. Enjoy the month and make good memories, for it holds out some special times indeed.

EDUCATION - Scholastic Luck

You have tremendous scholastic luck. Seize the initiative to engage in new learning opportunities. The energies of the month are particularly conducive to young Roosters pursuing knowledge and educating themselves. Enhance this kind of luck by turning on a **bright light** in the West sector of your study room. This will help crystallize things for you and may even gain you a scholarship if you are applying for one.

SECOND MONTH
March 6th - April 4th 2014

HIGH ENERGY LEVELS MAKE YOU ESPECIALLY PRODUCTIVE

The good things that came into your life last month carry on having their positive effects, keeping you busy, happy and fulfilled. The number 9 magnification star also serves to give you a boost in energy levels, allowing you to continue to make progress in your chosen pursuits. Success comes easily with few if any obstacles to slow you down. You are on a roll and should take advantage of the good energies to advance whatever you are putting your heart and mind to. Relationships benefit from your positive and buoyant attitude. You possess great influence over those in your circles, thus are able to motivate others to adopt and support your causes. As a boss, your staff look up to you; as a peer, your colleagues appreciate your manner and are so happy to work with you. There is a lot to look forward to!

WORK & CAREER - Professional Overdrive

There is lots happening at work and some of you could be on some kind of professional overdrive. You have stores of energy, but sometimes you will find your mind working much quicker than you physically are able.

Do take some time out to look after your health. Your life force and spirit essence are not at their height this year, so it is important not to take your good health for granted. Besides, you will also find that you are more productive when you give yourself some kind of structure to how you work, rather than diving into multiple tasks at once.

You are popular amongst those you work with, and if you mean to make an effective team, chances are you will. Do not try to do everything yourself; if you share out the work, you could find the sum adds up to more than the parts. Those of you involved in work that you are passionate about can achieve some truly great things this month.

BUSINESS - Effective Teamwork

This looks to be quite an awesome month for Roosters in business. You have your hands full yet you want to take on some more. You are passionate about the things you are involved in, but some of you may be tempted to take on yet more. There is no harm and in fact, the more you can cope with, the more success you can find. However, do not let it be at the expense of your health. Work at being an effective leader; the more efficient the teamwork in your operations, the more you can achieve with less effort. You will find plenty to smile about in your personal life as well, so if you free up some time, you will not have trouble filling it.

LOVE & RELATIONSHIPS - Passion

The heat gets turned up when it comes to your love life, but don't let the passion get out of hand. You will be in the mood for romance, and it is easy to get swept off your feet with the energies surrounding you at this time. Give in to your desires by all means, but don't let them to lead you to doing foolish things. It could pay to pace yourself somewhat rather than going full steam ahead. The single Roosters among you may be tempted to commit to a new relationship, but if it is with the wrong person, you could find it much more difficult to disentangle yourself. Avoid love triangles and other such "complicated" situations, because you really do not need to get yourself into this kind of trouble right now. Those of you married should direct some attention to your marriage, or infidelities could creep in.

EDUCATION - Excess Energy

You are feeling turbo-charged. Those of you who can effectively channel this energy into focused study can achieve quite awesome success. But the energies of the month could also make you more restless, with your mind wandering off when you should be concentrating.

THIRD MONTH
April 5th - May 5th 2014

YOUR RUN OF GOOD LUCK CONTINUES WITH THE WEALTH STAR VISITING

Another great month lies before you. Your go-getting temperament is tempered a little but this is a good thing; because it causes you to pause and think before diving in headfirst. You have had a tendency to be quite impulsive in the past few weeks, and this month you may have a reality check, reminding you to act with your head as well as your heart. This actually results in you making much better decisions. While you have been riding the wave of good fortune – which has led to some great things you might otherwise not have pursued – now it is time to take stock of where you are and make a strategic plan for the future. Be industrious but be clever about it.

WORK & CAREER - Making a Great Impression

Things are going great in many areas of your life, and this happiness translates into better productivity and performance at work. You are in a good mood and others appreciate that about you. They find you easy to work with and indeed actively seek you out. Your popularity at work also helps your chances in view of your career path; others have only good things to say about you, giving you a good reputation even with those who do not have everyday interaction with you. Contribute your ideas with confidence; even if not all of them are met with the same level of approval and praise, there will be quite a few that get picked up. You can make a noticeable difference in your organization if you set out to do just that. But watch you don't start stepping on any toes in your jostle to get ahead. If you make one of your main goals to ensure everyone stays on your side, you are setting yourself up to some remarkable success this year.

BUSINESS* - *Deal Making

This is a good month for dealmaking. You have a riveting effect on others, and new acquaintances like you instantly. Your charm will be apparent to most people you have dealings with, which makes you very successful in the business arena. A lot of people want to work with you merely because they like you. This is also a great month to invest and expand. You enjoy growth luck and the things you nurture now will bear fruit in the months to come. If there is anything you would like to change in your operations, this is a suitable time. Only make definite changes when your luck is on an upswing, otherwise the consequences could be dismal. But your luck is definitely looking good, so there is very little you need to worry about.

LOVE & RELATIONSHIPS - Romantic

Your capacity for love increases this month. You have much nurturing to do and if you have found someone to take care of, that person is lucky indeed. You are more emotionally in tune and will tend to be something of a romantic. This is not a time for casual romances. Beware when you take that approach, for you will be the one that ends up getting hurt. If you cannot have a future with someone, it is better not to get involved in the first place. But having said that, there is no harm in enjoying the wonders of love. The more total your idea of love is, the greater the experiences you will encounter.

EDUCATION - Seeing Results

This is a good month for learning. Continue working hard and you will start to see results materializing. It is easy to achieve top grades if you constantly work at it, and when you start achieving big, it does not seem hard at all. Once you fit yourself into an effective routine, it gives you a buzz. When you start to enjoy your studies this way, there is no end then to what you can accomplish.

FENG SHUI ENHANCER: Wear the **Infinity Symbol** to enhance the positive energies of the wealth and prosperity star this month.

FOURTH MONTH
May 6th - June 5th 2014

EXCESS OF METAL ENERGY BRINGS SOME DANGER

The number 7 violent star flies into your home sector, joining the annual number 6 star. Together, these two stars create an excess of Metal energy, and while this may bolster the Rooster's intrinsic element of Metal, it could also cause you to make reckless decisions and to act before you think. Safety also becomes an issue this month; the number 7 star brings risk of robbery, theft, money loss and betrayal. Not nice things, although you can go some way to nullifying its ill effects with suitable feng shui cures.

Ensure the West of your home has a **pair of Blue Rhinos** to quash the risk of robbery, especially if there is a door in the West. Install a **water feature** in this part of your home also, which will exhaust the precarious Metal energy. This is a month when you need to watch your back. Don't give your trust too easily, be careful with unknown quantities, and avoid taking any risks.

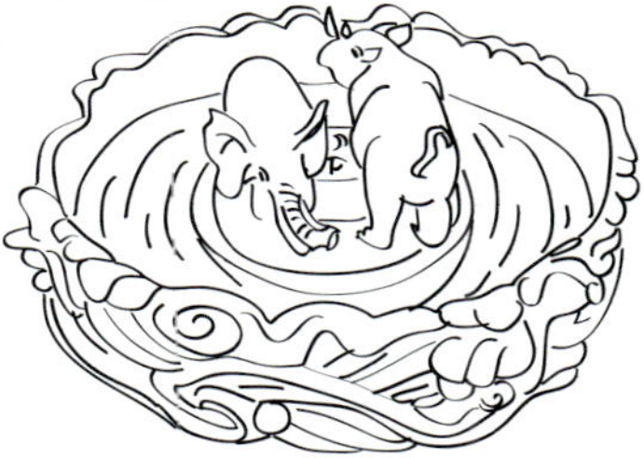

WORK & CAREER - ***Keep a Low Profile***

Try to keep a low profile this month. Do not engage in challenges. Avoid lengthy discussions where the chance of a disagreement could crop up. This is not a time to be controversial or divisive. You are in need of allies, so nurture your friendships in the workplace. Do not ruffle any feathers or they could be your undoing. Continue working hard or your slacking will be noticed immediately. Think defensive rather than offensive. There is some danger of being played out, so do watch what you say and who you say it to. It is better to play your cards close to your chest. There is no need to share your honest thoughts about everything, even if your opinion is asked for. This month it is better to play the diplomat, or even the politician.

BUSINESS - ***Obstacles***

There may be some sizeable obstacles to overcome this month. After things have been going so smoothly over the past few months, any scent of trouble could faze you, but do not let yourself get immobilized. Approach each problem that crops up individually, and solve them one at a time. If an issue is a big one, break it up and approach it step by step. There is also no need to feel that you have to face challenges alone. Tap the brains of your team. Confide in them and welcome their ideas. You may discover a jewel in your staff you never knew you had. Facing some tough times together may bring more benefits than setbacks, if it forges an even greater alliance between you and your staff.

LOVE & RELATIONSHIPS* - *Not in the Mood

A small disagreement or misunderstanding with your partner could arise, and if not nipped in the bud could grow into something bigger and more deep-seated. Sort out any problems you have as soon as you are able and try to be bighearted about it. Be generous in spirit and don't hold on to false ideals. Something that applied long ago may not apply now because your relationship has changed. If neither of you backs down, you could do some irreparable damage to your relationship. It could even lead to separation. Don't play games with each other. In the end, you will both lose out. The single Rooster is unlikely to find this a conducive month to pursue a new romance. You are generally not in the mood, and this could put some people off.

PERSONAL SAFETY* - *Be More Careful

The number 7 star is a violent star and brings with it risk to your personal safety. Be more careful when you are out and about, and ladies especially, should not stay out late alone. Carry the **Night Safety Amulet** and don't take any chances. Things need only go wrong one time.

FIFTH MONTH
June 6th - July 6th 2014

UNSEEN HAND HELPING YOU MAKE GOOD DECISIONS

Things start to proceed smoothly for you again. The heavenly month star joins the heavenly annual star, helping things fall into place. Problems that were irking you quite literally evaporate into thin air without you having to do too much. You get help from all the right people, allowing you to pursue your ambitions and objectives. You are on a winning team and others want to be on it, so when they offer their help, don't feel bad about taking it. The situations work themselves out to be win-win, so all parties benefit. Be generous when you achieve success and more will come to you. This is a time when your inner voice holds power. Give in to your instincts and go with your heart, because you possess an innate wisdom that drives you to do and say all the right things. You also become more energized, allowing you to take on more than before. This aspect of your luck is particularly appreciated, as the Rooster person is always happiest when there is too much to get done.

Carry the **Heaven Luck Activator** to make the most of your good fortune this month.

☺

WORK & CAREER - *Definite Direction*
You could be handed an attractive challenge at work. More responsibilities may be expected of you but there is definite direction when it comes to carving out a good career path for yourself. There could be talk of where your future is headed in the company. You get along especially well with your boss and superiors this month, and they are in just the right position to help you further yourself in your career. Look out for opportunities to use your skill sets to the best of your ability. Seize the initiative when it comes to offering your expertise. Doing more than is expected of you will bode well for your future, and will be particularly effective at this time.

BUSINESS - *Pursuing New Opportunities*
There are many opportunities to pursue, all of which are perfectly achievable with the right resources and with assistance from the right people. This is a time when you may have to call on friends to open some doors for you. It is well worth asking for small favours; and you will find many who are only too willing to help you. They may want a slice of the pie, but the more you can make it worth their while, the better the quality of help they can offer. Get others on your team. Roosters who build an effective side will do far better than those who prefer to work alone. This could be a good time to enter into a mutually beneficial partnership.

LOVE & RELATIONSHIPS - *Be Bold*

Things are extremely positive for the Rooster looking for romance. Single Roosters have a great possibility to find a true soul mate if you are actively looking. The *Heavenly Star* brings luck in love as much as luck in work and business. The next four weeks are about pursuing your dreams and then achieving them, and matters of the heart are by no means excluded. If you focus your energies on what you want, you find it quite easily.

Be a little bit bold when going after what you want. Do not wait until the perfect moment to announce your intentions. If you wait too long, the ship may have sailed. Don't wait to be pursued; do some pursuing yourself. Stay secure and don't let self-doubt creep in. Even if you may not know if someone likes you back, take a chance. If they feel the same way, you may have found yourself something magical, and if they don't, you can keep on looking.

EDUCATION - *Mentor Luck*

The young Rooster, above all things, enjoys superb mentor luck this month. This makes it a shame if you do not have someone you can go to for help, advice or guidance. If you don't have anybody like this, you may want to start looking. You will benefit tremendously.

SIXTH MONTH
July 7th - Aug 7th 2014

MISFORTUNE FIVE YELLOW THROWS A SPANNER INTO THE WORKS

Not really a good time. This is one of your unluckier months of the year, so it pays to be more careful. There may be small misfortunes on the cards, but you cope well as long as you keep up your mental strength. Do not crumble in the face of minor disappointments. Letting a small setback become a big issue in your life will only lead it to blow up into something bigger. When others ask for help, give it willingly and happily. There could be opportunities beckoning, but because this is an unlucky month, it is better to wait till next month to act on new opportunities. Ventures started now have little chance of success in the long run. Those of you still studying could find this a tiring month. Do not let exhaustion catch up with you by ensuring you get enough rest and sleep between work assignments.

WORK & CAREER - Office Politics

The coming month brings some dissatisfaction at the workplace, but your best plan of action is to lie low and swallow humilities if need be. Your personal store of luck is running low, and if you raise a challenge, chances of you losing out are high. Suppress the cocky Rooster spirit in you, or you could see a great loss of position and influence. Delay plans you may have to show off your skills and talents. The less you appear to show-off, the less you stand to lose. There could be politicking at the office, and don't be surprised if a great deal is aimed at you. You may be an easy target, but responding will only make it easier for your adversaries. Carry the **Anti-Office Politics Amulet** to deflect their efforts. The mood at work improves markedly next month, but for now, keep a low profile and just get on with the real work.

***BUSINESS** - Keep Things Going As Usual*

Roosters in business should try to keep business going as usual as far as possible. Maintain the status quo. If you have a tried and tested formula, don't start to change things now. This is no time to be experimenting with new ideas, because even if they are good, things can easily go wrong when you don't know exactly what you are doing and your luck is down. Avoid investing, expanding or trying anything out of the ordinary. Maintain a close watch on your cash flow as you could have some unexpected expenses to cover. There may be some staff problems to deal with, but try not to blow things out of proportion. The bigger you make a problem in your head, the worse it gets. Some things are not solvable immediately, but if you can wait till next month when your luck improves, you are likely to make a positive difference.

LOVE & ROMANCE - *No Need to Win*

There is change on the cards when it comes to love and relationships for the Rooster. Be prepared for a transitional period ahead. Some of you may find that your relationship has run its course. If you are no longer happy, it may be time to move on. Don't prolong the break-up period if this is the case. The young Rooster in love has the ability to pick up the pieces and start afresh very quickly, so don't keep looking back to the past.

Those of you who are married or in stable steady relationships may find misunderstandings arise more often this month. Back off arguments and don't let small disagreements become more than they are. If you know you have something good, do everything in your power to hold on to it. Don't react in anger. Give yourself time to cool off and recompose yourself before trying to win an argument. And remember that at times like these, winning is not necessarily a victory. In love, sometimes it is better to lose.

SEVENTH MONTH
Aug 8th - Sept 7th 2014

RELATIONSHIPS BRING YOU MUCH JOY THIS MONTH

The unique way the stars have combined in your chart causes love luck to blossom. The romantic number 4 star combines with the resident 6 to form a *sum-of-ten,* bringing you happiness and success with another person. Romance characterizes the next few weeks, causing those of you who have been looking to finally find the real thing. There is marriage on the cards for some Roosters, or a serious relationship may begin for others. Those of you already in steady relationships will find your partners featuring in a big way this month. You gain much from being bonded to a special someone, whether as lovers or soul mates. Strong partnerships are the key to moving forward. There is little to come in the way of your happiness so you can look forward to a joyful four weeks.

WORK & CAREER - Feeling Positive

You are in a highly positive frame of mind, which puts you in a good mood at work. Your lively disposition makes you popular amongst those you work with, and you make an excellent member of any team. Others find it easy and very pleasant to work with you. There are many opportunities but some of them will involve a choice. Go with your heart when deciding on anything that will affect your future; if you listen to your own inner voice, you will not go too far wrong.

For some of you, there is a possibility of a romance blossoming from a contact you meet through work. Those of you who dedicate a big part of your life to your job could start to yearn companionship, and if your life has become your work, those who excite you are those with the most in common with you – your work. Watch however that you do not get romantically involved with the wrong person, or there could be trouble. Do not jeopardize your future for no reason.

BUSINESS - Hands On

Fortunate meetings lead to new acquaintances that can advance your position. Develop the relationships you make; they will form an important network of contacts for things you will be doing in the near future. Your business story now will depend much on your people skills and personality. This is a time when your natural charm and way with words will get you far. Be hands on when dealing with associates and clients. They will appreciate the personal touch. This is a time to think long term. Even if you cannot immediately see any short term benefit to contacts you nurture now, they come in useful later on.

LOVE & RELATIONSHIPS - *Magical*

This is a magical time for the Rooster looking for love. You are starry-eyed and idealistic, making you delightful company. If you are single, there will be quite a few people vying for your attention and affection. While this is flattering, you are not so interested in relationships that you don't think can last or have a future. Even if you are not yet with anyone, thoughts of marriage and beyond are probably already crossing your mind, especially those of you with friends who have seemingly idyllic family lives. The *Peach Blossom Star* in your chart, when activated, can bring marriage luck very quickly. Your *Peach Blossom* animal is the **Horse**; to activate for marriage luck, display a beautiful image of a horse in the South of your home.

EDUCATION - *Achievement-Oriented*

The number 4 star is also the *Scholastic Star*, and when it combines with the number 6, as it does this month, it forms the most auspicious *sum-of-ten* combination which brings success and completion luck. Some of you will start consolidating what you know, leading to everything falling nicely into place for you.

EIGHTH MONTH
Sept 8th - Oct 7th 2014

A QUARRELSOME TIME FOR THE ROOSTER

The number 3 star brings difficult energies into your chart, making your relationships tense and your mood more irritable. You have a short fuse and do not have the patience for those who cannot see things from your point of view. Discussions become agitated affairs and it is easy to make some unnecessary enemies with your flippant tongue. This month it is better to keep a low profile and not to say too much. Working with others becomes more difficult. For some of you, litigation and problems with the authorities bring tension and stress. This is a time when it is best to lie low and to avoid drawing unwanted attention to yourself. Watch also who you offend because those who become unwitting victims of your temper could plot their own petty revenge. Calm the energies of the month by carrying the **Peace & Harmony Amulet**.

WORK & CAREER - *Altercations*

This is an argumentative month when you may find yourself getting into altercations with colleagues. Your subordinates may annoy you with their incompetence, and your bosses may seem unfair in your eyes. But this is not the time to make known any ill-feelings towards others as they are likely to be misconstrued. These negative thoughts will evaporate soon enough, but for now do try to work at keeping your temper in check. Losing your cool will only lose your friends, face and credibility. The best strategy for you now is not to take on too much. Work hard, but avoid situations which put you up against others. Avoid group discussions that are controversial, and keep a **Singing Bowl** nearby to clear the air around you each time you feel anger begin to well up inside you.

BUSINESS - Keep Your Cool

Not a smooth-sailing time ahead. There are obstacles that threaten to derail your plans. Others may not be on the same page as you, making it difficult to have coherent discussions. There will be moments when it seems that all the hard work you have put in has gone to waste. Even if something you have been working on does not come to anything, if you adopt the right attitude, you can learn from it. Nothing is wasted if you maintain the correct mindset. Your temper could make you some temporary enemies; if you realize this, take immediate action to rectify the situation, or you could end up causing a chain of events that leads to something perfectly avoidable.

LOVE & RELATIONSHIPS - *Difficult*

This could be a difficult month when it comes to relationships. While you are incredibly charming with people you are not that close to, you could find yourself losing patience with your nearest and dearest. This does nothing for your relationship, and could well drive your partner into the arms of someone else.

Beware the threat of the *Star of External Romance;* its presence this year looms large, particularly for those in rocky relationships. While your love life may not be "rocky", this month could see you saying some hurtful things. Hold your tongue or you risk doing some irreparable damage. Not a good time to plan for important events, and particularly avoid marriages, engagements and other such celebrations during this time.

EDUCATION - *Keep Calm*

There may seem more for you to do than usual. More assignments and more deadlines to meet. Don't let these run up your stress levels, or you will find it even more difficult to complete your work. Stay emotionally calm. Even if there is a lot to get done, give yourself a break once in a while. A holiday would do you a world of good.

NINTH MONTH
Oct 8th - Nov 6th 2014

SUSCEPTIBLE TO ILL HEALTH THIS MONTH

Illness prevails so you need to watch your health. The number 2 illness star has flown into your chart, causing you to fall sick more easily. You are susceptible to the common cold, flu and temperature change. You could also be plagued by headaches and migraines. If you are feeling under the weather, try and take it easy. This is not the time to start new ventures or to pursue new things. It is better used for consolidation and retrospection. You find yourself more thoughtful and pensive. Your brainpower is strong though your physical body may be weaker than usual. Use this time to plan and strategize. There is lots of time later for pursuing your dreams and acting on your ideas, but this is not the time. More than half the battle is usually won in the planning, so it is by no means a do-nothing month. Instead, remain stealthy and in touch, watchful but non-obvious.

WORK & CAREER - Turn on the Charm

Plan your work before jumping into things, and you will find yourself more efficient and doing the job better. Cooperation is important this month. Working well

☹

with others will help you complete your tasks more quickly, more professionally and more impressively. If you try to do everything alone, you could land yourself in some hot water. If you are unsure about something, it is far better to ask. You could find yourself in certain situations that call for great diplomacy. Use your charisma to win others over. When you make up your mind to get others on your side, you are usually successful. Don't let your impatience and arrogance ruin things for you.

BUSINESS - Plan Now Act Later

This is a month to solidify your current strengths, rather than looking for ways to diversify. Delay plans for expansion and instead look at how you can improve the way you currently run your business. Any planning and strategy work done now will lead to rewards later on, but do not act impulsively. Make tentative decisions on your next move, but refrain from acting on that move till next month. This month is one for contemplating the past and improving yourself for the future. Strengthen your team by boosting team spirit. Share your goals with your staff and get everyone on the same page; but make sure no one acts prematurely or your plan could go awry. Opportunities may present themselves through a long-lost acquaintance. Listen to ideas with an open mind, but wait till next month before you act.

LOVE & RELATIONSHIPS - *Special Times*

There is a lot of love on the horizon. For the single Rooster, the coming month could see you meeting someone who will light your fire and bring new romance into your life. Together you can share many activities and experiences. Don't fall for the first person who woos you because there are a lot better things coming. You will know you have found the One when there is a true meeting of minds. The Rooster personality will never be satisfied in a shallow relationship with a partner who is not your intellectual match. In general, when it comes to love relationships, the next four weeks promise a good time. For those of you who are married, your love for your spouse grows, especially if you make an effort to nurture your relationship.

EDUCATION - *Step-by-Step*

You may have dreams and ideals, but remember to keep one foot on the ground. While you may have lofty ambitions, it makes sense to aim at something attainable for now. Break up your ultimate goals up into steps. This will help you stay motivated. Rejoice in all the small achievements because these are what will lead you to the big ones later on.

TENTH MONTH
Nov 7th - Dec 6th 2014

HO TU BRINGS NEW OPPORTUNITIES FOR LEARNING

The number 1 star joins with the heaven star in your chart, strengthening this *Ho Tu* combination to bring you luck in education and learning. All of those of you striving to improve yourselves can achieve a lot this coming month. Remember that you can learn from more than one source. While you may respect certain teachers for certain skills, don't close your mind to learning in other ways as well. This is a time when you gain not only in new knowledge but in wisdom also. Look on all your experiences as life lessons. If you spend some time contemplating, revelations will start to dawn on you, giving you a much clearer picture of what you want to do and where you want to be. A fulfilling time for those of you who pause to take stock of your situation.

WORK & CAREER - Making Good Progress

You make good progress at work. There are good opportunities for you to learn new things and to expand your skill set. Those of you who open your mind up to learning will get a lot more out of the month than those who think they know it all. Be humble and appreciative when someone tries to help you. Take advice with the right attitude. Don't look on suggestions as criticism; even if not everything you do is met with enthusiasm, try to learn from it and improve. Make good friends with your co-workers; impressing the boss is one thing, but the more people you have on your side, the more pleasant your career path will be. Even for those of you who are ambitious about progressing quickly up the career ladder, there is no need to trample others down to get there. If you are gracious and helpful you will find the reciprocity more than proportionate in your favour.

BUSINESS - *Going Great Guns*

Things in business are looking up for the Rooster! There are plenty of new opportunities opening up, many of which are truly exciting. Even if you are not completely familiar with processes or what you may find yourself getting into, stay confident. You learn up new things quickly, and you may even have an advantage from approaching it from an outsider's perspective. You get the chance to break into new industries and to diversify your business at a time when expansion in the same direction may have reached saturation point. The more creative you are, and the more open to new ideas, the better you will do. The month really does have a lot to offer. Do not waste your good fortune when everything comes together so nicely. Be pro-active and follow up on your leads.

LOVE & RELATIONSHIPS - Love Blossoms

A wonderful time for the Rooster pursuing romance! There are multiple new discoveries to be made, and for those of you in new relationships, you will find getting to know your partner better a heavenly experience. Take the lead when it comes to your relationship. There is no need to follow convention. Go where others have not gone before. You can afford to be different about the way you approach life, love and relationships. As long as you remain true to yourself, there are so many beautiful ways for love to blossom for you this month.

Those of you who are married or in steady relationships will find new ways to appreciate your partner. Spend as much time nurturing your marriage as you do cultivating outside relationships and you will see the immense value of family.

EDUCATION - New Discoveries

What a wonderful time for the young Rooster! There are new discoveries to be made and your capacity for learning expands far beyond even your own expectations. Spend more time with those who focus on your strengths and achievements. You may have envious peers who may try to make you feel bad about yourself. Stay far away from them.

ELEVENTH MONTH
Dec 7th 2014 - Jan 5th 2015

A BUSY TIME AS THE FESTIVE SEASON SETS IN

You will find yourself with little time to think this month. You are always on the go, and each day passes too quickly. Although it will seem like you will never get everything done, things fall into place nicely. In fact it will be the busiest among you Roosters who will be the happiest. You may experience some stressful moments, but it is not a bad kind of stress. It is one that comes with other positive feelings of achievement and triumph. There is definitely a competitive spirit in you, which makes you excel in activities and endeavours where there is a strong competitive element. It being year-end as well, with the Christmas and New Year festivities coming up, you will find your social life as busy if not more so than your work and family life. An excellent opportunity to network and to strengthen and deepen your relationships with acquaintances, who can easily become good friends.

WORK & CAREER - Persuasive

There is plenty going on at work, but your assignments are of a most enjoyable kind. You excel with tasks that involve interaction with others, especially when it involves convincing them round to your point of view. You are very persuasive in the way you converse, making you a master negotiator. This skill of yours comes in as useful for yourself when discussing you bonus package with your boss as it does when selling a new product or service to a client or customer.

You are doing very well indeed and the feng shui stars in your chart are in your favour. Mentor luck is enhanced by the visiting magnification star of 9; this brings you help and good guidance from those you consider your mentors. There are also unseen forces helping you make wise decisions. Do not be afraid to follow your heart at this time; your instincts are good and your passion is paramount.

BUSINESS - Good Publicity

This is a good month for Roosters in business. There is a lot happening and you could find yourself in the news. Make the best of the publicity you are getting. This is a great time for new openings and new launches. Marketing initiatives bring great returns and your target audience are receptive to your message. Have a clear and focused marketing strategy; people are listening to what you say, so make sure you are telling them something worthwhile. Within your operations, make a greater effort to get to know your staff better. Apply your knowledge even in areas of the business you have been leaving in the hands of your managers. However excellent they may be, they can benefit greatly from your input at this time.

LOVE & RELATIONSHIPS - In the Mood

Do not neglect your personal life in the midst of a hectic work life; especially important if you are married with a family. You will be in the mood for romance, so direct all this energy towards your partner and not outside to some third party. Beware office romances and infidelities brought on by too many drinks at work parties. The repercussions may be severe if you succumb. Carry the **Anti-infidelity Amulet** this month to protect against untoward happenings of this kind. This will also help ensure that your spouse does not fall victim to the *Star of External Romance* either.

The single Rooster can look forward to an active month when it comes to romance, but should follow similar advice to their married counterparts. Do not succumb to office romances or one night stands, and do not get involved with unsuitable partners such as those already married. You would be setting yourself up for disappointment and heartache. You have a lot better things in store for you than that, so don't fall into a trap!

TWELFTH MONTH
Jan 6th - Feb 3rd 2015

DIVINE MONTH WHEN INDICATIONS ARE VERY POSITIVE

The prosperity star makes an appearance bringing new wealth luck. Some of you could benefit from a windfall of some kind; through a bonus payment, an inheritance, an unexpected gift or even a lottery win. There are very positive energies about, so make sure you enjoy yourself. The people around you are very supportive, and those of you in management positions will find your team looking up to you in great admiration. Accept help offered to you graciously, even if you may not think you need any help. Others flock to you, drawn by your charisma and magnetism. It is an easy time for making new friends, and to develop the friendships you already have. Make time for others who are seeking your time. If you can help somebody, do it. Even if you have to inconvenience yourself a little, it will mean a lot more to them than you know. Pay it forward and good things will come back to you very quickly.

WORK & CAREER - Tempting Opportunities

Chances are you will be feeling very satisfied with where you are at with work. Your career is going well. Some of you may be approached with new opportunities from outside of your current job, but before you jump ship and make any critical decisions, consider your options carefully. Do not make rash decisions you could regret without first thinking things through. You should also consult your family and those close to you before making choices that will affect them also.

While some opportunities may seem too good to be missed, look also at the downsides of taking them up, and the upsides of staying put where you are. Your ultimate choice will depend on your individual situation, but as long as you give yourself time to analyze your options, you will end up making the right decisions. Just don't let your head get turned, leading you to act impulsively and possibly foolishly.

BUSINESS* - *Growth Luck

This is a great month to invest and expand. You enjoy fabulous growth luck. Things that get started now hold much promise for the future. Be confident when making plans and acting on them. You have many new ideas you would like to implement. Spend some effort to get a task force in place to carry out these ideas, and don't sit on them for too long. This month favours action when you have something good up your sleeve. The quicker you can get things going, the better. Be sure to have everything well on its way by the end of the month, because next month is one when you need to stay cautious again. Be sure to lay all the ground work now.

LOVE & RELATIONSHIPS - *Fabulous*

A wonderful time for love and matters of the heart. Your relationship with your partner gets a boost from the loving energies of the month, and you will find that the more you confide in each other, the more supportive you will find one another. It will also deepen your bonds and make your union stronger and more meaningful. Those of you in new relationships will be thinking forward to taking things to the next level. This is a lucky month for proposals, getting engaged and getting married. Such happiness occasions will also serve to augment your already excellent luck further.

EDUCATION - *Conducive to Learning*

The young Rooster benefits from the positive energies of the month, which will make learning more fruitful and more satisfying. There are some exciting new directions opening up for some of you. A beneficial time for you to pursue them.

PART FOUR

FENG SHUI OF THE ROOSTER'S LOVE LIFE IN 2014

Prospects for love, romance & marriage looking incredibly good

In 2014, the Rooster's love relationships go through a good year for those still in the dating game and looking for a mate. The Rooster in search of a life partner will experience excitement and positive expectation as good potential partners enter your life. The Horse sign is the Rooster's Peach Blossom animal, and since this is the Year of the Horse with the Peach Blossom Star number of 4 dominating the year's energies in the center, this gives Rooster's love life an incredible boost. Thus for those hoping to get married this year, the prospects for doing so look good.

COMPATIBILITY WITH EACH ANIMAL SIGN

COMPATIBILITY	LUCK OUTLOOK IN 2014
ROOSTER with RAT	Cozy ambience of shared ambitions
ROOSTER with OX	A pair that is hard to beat
ROOSTER with TIGER	Clash of wills
ROOSTER with RABBIT	A good match through good times and bad
ROOSTER with DRAGON	Great affinity
ROOSTER with SNAKE	A Pairing made in heaven!
ROOSTER with HORSE	Empowering one another in 2014
ROOSTER with SHEEP	Good humour will help this union
ROOSTER with MONKEY	Blissful at first but you may tire of each other
ROOSTER with ROOSTER	Two self-centered individuals could find a pairing between them difficult
ROOSTER with DOG	Little understanding between this pair
ROOSTER with BOAR	Bringing out the best in each other

For those already in a committed relationship or married, the year brings some excitement but also the possibility of betrayals. This is a year when the married Rooster can succumb to the *Star of External Romance*, having to cope with emotional complications aggravating your life. Some of you might get hurt.

It is a yang year, and since the Rooster is a yin sign, this is not a bad year to focus on the romantic side of your life.

Your sign is sure to benefit from relationship success because of the 4 in the center of the year's feng shui chart. This puts focus on your love life. But it is not all smooth sailing as there will be competitive pressures in your love relationships.

The Rooster benefits from getting support and introductions from unexpected quarters and those of you who are already in a stable relationship or are married will find the year quite exhausting. The extent of your aggravations depends on the animal sign you are married to, but many of you will simply take comfort in domesticity as this will suit your temperament and expectations this year. Rooster men and women continue to depend on their superb skill of managing their feelings. Troubles within a family headed by a

Rooster father or mother get dealt with efficiently and without too much drama. The Rooster woman is likely to be bossy and down-to-earth, while the Rooster patriarch is likely to indulge his roving eye potential. Rooster men do not think twice about being unfaithful to their wives, but you should this year - otherwise complications that will drag into the long term could cause you no end of problems.

Rooster men rarely wear their hearts on their sleeves and those among you who have a tendency to cheat will usually be also very good at staying low key about your affairs, which is just as well, since being too honest will simply get you into trouble.

The Rooster exudes an air of dependability, which colleagues and family find reassuring. This also applies to the Rooster lady, who is as close-mouthed as her male counterpart. Those still single will be very willing to "commit" to any new love relationship and there will be no shortage of "suitors".

The good news is that the Rooster is pretty much "in charge" in any of your love relationships whether you are male or female. You handle your love life with great efficiency and you have a good grip on your emotions.

Thus although 2014 is a year when you might succumb to the reducing energy star, still you will rarely let your heart completely rule your head.

The Rooster is not as vulnerable as many of the other signs, but you will still need to be careful that you do not get entangled in emotional complications.

Note that when confronted with precocious situations, you can find yourself at a loss as to how to manage your affairs. In any case, you are not strong in this Year of the Horse and you are not prepared for the different kinds of feelings that will manifest for you.

These days, the social scene is full of predatory females who stalk successful men as well as unscrupulous men who go after successful women. You are not as immune to temptations as you may like to believe.

The single Rooster wishing to find a soulmate or trigger marriage luck can try using the powerful method of activating **Peach Blossom Marriage Luck.** Using your animal sign as a guide, this method works best during a year when the intensity of the Peach

Blossom is enhanced with the number 4 in the center of the feng shui chart.

In years such as 2014, Peach Blossom enhancements work within three months, bringing you the kind of love that can lead to marriage. The Peach Blossom ritual also works for those of you who have been going steady but with one partner unwilling to commit or set the date. But there is also the *External Star of Romance* this year, so there could be complications in your love life!

ACTIVATING FOR MARRIAGE LUCK

To activate your Peach Blossom, that is, to find love that leads to marriage, the Rooster-born person should activate the **South corner** of your bedroom by placing **horses** there – the more robust and feisty, and the more valuable and beautiful the horses look, the better will be the potential husband or wife you attract as your spouse.

Place painted horses or look for gem-encrusted horses to display in the South of your most frequently-used rooms. Make sure not to get cheap-looking horse images from roadside stalls or shops that look rundown. And make sure you buy from someone who makes you feel good! The energy associated with the Peach Blossom animal must be creative and classy.

PEACH BLOSSOM SYMBOLS

Your PEACH BLOSSOM animal placed in the center activates ROMANCE luck

RABBIT

is the PEACH BLOSSOM for

HORSE
TIGER
DOG

HORSE

is the PEACH BLOSSOM for

ROOSTER
SNAKE
OX

The chart showing the PEACH BLOSSOM ANIMALS for the 12 animal signs

True love will manifest in different ways for each of the five kinds of Rooster-born, but it comes when you activate your Peach Blossom animal.

Also examine your love luck with each of the twelve signs of the Zodiac and check out how you will react with those near and dear to you this year.

FOR THE 12 ANIMAL SIGNS

ROOSTER

is the PEACH BLOSSOM for

DRAGON
MONKEY
RAT

RAT

is the PEACH BLOSSOM for

RABBIT
SHEEP
BOAR

ROOSTER/RAT

Cozy ambience of shared ambitions

Between the Rooster and Rat can easily develop a love/hate relationship that blows hot and cold. But there is genuine attraction and love can easily develop so that eventually a pretty deep relationship can get formed. And yet this can also be something of a mismatch, as you are both so different.

The Rooster and Rat can go on for weeks quarrelling over the most inconsequential of matters and often it will be you, the Rooster, who will be unrelenting in wanting to win all the arguments. In truth though, both of you are equally to blame in the battle of wits you play with each other. The Rat's hard-headedness annoys the Rooster, and yet when you make up, there is more than enough goodwill generated to take you through some days before you are at it again.

In 2014 however, the Rooster's air of superiority softens and the Rat responds with grace. Both of you enjoy powerful *Ho Tu* combinations that bring large and lucky distractions. The Rat's *Ho Tu* of 4/9 brings wonderfully stimulating business luck. Commercial ventures succeed easily and smoothly, taking the Rat to new heights of ambition. This situation is very pleasing to the Rooster, thus creating a cozy ambience of shared ambitions. The year will be kind to you both, bringing a lovely feeling of contentment amidst great and meaningful activity. But the Rooster also benefits from its own *Ho Tu* of 1/6, a combination that creates the cosmic element of Water. Here the Ho Tu is not in its waxing cycle, but it brings cosmic water, which makes up for it being missing from the basket of elements this year. Thus while this combination brings scholastic brilliance and academic success, in 2014 it also brings power, recognition and rank. This indicates that in this relationship, it will be the Rooster who holds the upper hand.

FENG SHUI TIP: You can even out the power balance between the two of you by placing a **Dragon image** in your bedroom; this will soften the Rooster (as the Dragon is its secret friend) and strengthen the Rat (as the Dragon is your astrological ally). The secrets of astrological influences can be powerful enhancing-agents, and for you both, it is the Dragon that enhances your charisma! The Dragon image is always beneficial for both your signs, but let it be a bejeweled Golden Dragon if you want it to benefit the Rooster more, and a **Blue Coiling Dragon** if you want to favour the Rat.

ROOSTER/OX

A pair that is hard to beat

The Rooster has a special connection with the Ox. You are astrological allies supporting each other spontaneously. Both are "reliable types" and any match forged between the two of you has a good chance of surviving even the most trying of circumstances.

You can be good friends for life or you can be in a love relationship or even married, but the main attribute of this match is the instinctive trust you will develop in each other. The Ox and Rooster are individualistic, but you get along because you have genuine respect for each other.

There is a practical down-to-earth attitude about the two of you that will take you very far as a couple. There is a synergy to your personalities and you hold deep trust for one another. In 2014, the Ox is very strong in terms of physical wellbeing and mental strength, while the Rooster is weak. Ox is at its peak and Rooster is at its lowest! This is a great disparity between the two of you in terms of your inner and outer strength. So there is a mismatch of energies. But the Ox will see the Rooster through the year with support and understanding. From this perspective, the match between the two of you is hard to beat.

The year's energy patterns cause the Rooster to suffer from the *Star of Reducing Energy* while the Ox is beset with feng shui obstacles caused by conflict and killing stars brought to its doorstep of Northeast by the cosmic forces of the year. This brings aggravations.

Together you will grow closer in 2014 because of these challenges. Yours is a home where everything works well, the efficient hand of the Rooster being clearly evident. There is also the steadiness of the Ox's influence. Both bring substantial value-added to the relationship. If meeting for the first time, you will fall in love easily and it will be a match made in heaven.

In the case of those of you who are married, the patient Ox puts up with Rooster's bossiness. There is acceptance and adaptation. Yours is a long term commitment that leads to a meaningful match.

The relationship between Ox and Rooster usually has every chance to succeed. Both benefit from auspicious Ho Tu combinations this year. There are some excellent developments bringing the both of you some very good news. Hence 2014 will be a happy year for you.

ROOSTER/TIGER
Clash of wills

The Tiger and Rooster are not naturally well-suited to each other and in fact, the two of you possess personalities that disturb each other's peace of mind. As lovers or partners living together, there is a constant clash of wills and both sides end up happy and yet also angry.

The Rooster, though symbolically smaller in size than the Tiger, and certainly not possessed of the Tiger's physical strength, is nevertheless just as fierce and domineering in character. In 2014 however, the Rooster is in a milder kind of mood, more than happy to compromise and humour the Tiger.

The Tiger is weak this year, but so is the Rooster. In terms of life force and Spiritual Essence these two signs have something significant in common - both are in need of good strong chi energy. But the Rooster enjoys excellent success luck this year, while the Tiger's success luck is low. The Rooster is also blessed by the presence of the *Heavenly Star* of 6, which brings heavenly blessings, while the Tiger is harmed by the wrathful star 7. This is a year of conflicts for the two of you. The Rooster must not be too demanding as the

Tiger will be in a quarrelsome mood. This relationship really requires hard work from both sides. There are conflict stars flanking both the Rooster and the Tiger in 2014, so there is plenty of conflict energy.

Neither will lean towards compromise nor want to put in the effort to make the relationship work. Neither wishes to endure the other's aggravations. The Tiger's physical strength can turn violent this year because of the number 7 star, and any outbreak of direct conflict will be ugly. For any Tiger/Rooster pairing that splits this year, there will be long-lasting bitterness. Ugly words create a permanent divide. Between these two, there is little hope of compromise once they become adversaries. Those in a relationship and going through tough times may want to consider parting amicably before things get really ugly.

In terms of your inner essence, the Tiger might find it useful to remember that your natural element is Wood while that of the Rooster's is Metal. In the cycle, Metal destroys Wood, so this can be potentially a destructive relationship, made really bad by the year's conflict stars. Better then to split!

ROOSTER/RABBIT

Spirituality finds you common ground

This pair of signs are described as the East/West astrological enemies of the Zodiac wheel; their locations and their personalities directly opposite and opposing to one another, but in 2014, they unite under heaven's luck directly emanating from the Rooster's largesse and the big influence of the powerful 1/6 Ho Tu, which brings wisdom and great learning as well. This year, heaven's blessings bring wonderful understanding, and even love, which can arise between these two signs.

The year smiles on this normally bad match of individuals. Most years the Rooster and Rabbit cannot find common ground, each put off by what they see as the other's moral righteousness. They cannot even hold a discussion without one getting impatient or abusive. There is little trust between them even when they are siblings or classmates! And amongst those of you who are pursuing only worldly wealth and worldly success find it hard to see any good in the other. There is no common ground on which you can build any kind of friendship, let alone an intimate relationship. It is only when one of you introduces the concept of spirituality into the relationship equation that something deeper and more subtle emerges. And then you begin to find common ground.

This year, the heavenly star 6 flies into the Rooster's sign, so that even with conflict stars flanking the Rooster and one conflict star influencing the Rabbit, heaven's blessing is powerful. The Rooster's weak life force and spiritual essence reveals its vulnerability and the Rabbit discover qualities in the Rooster you were previously blind to. Pull aside the veil of human concerns and go beyond the cosmic; that is when you, the Rooster will see Rabbitwith new eyes.

Those meeting for the first time will be slow to trust but once a relationship gets forged, you will overlook superficial differences between you. Tolerance replaces annoyance, and indulgence takes the place of narrow-mindedness. Whether or not you can last as a couple depends on you individually. You need to transcend and look beyond life's lower chakra aspirations and pursue instead your path into spirituality; otherwise you are unlikely to last as a couple. Too many small grievances build up to make you to succumb to the astrological forces that divide you. But for 2014, you get along surprisingly well. Those already married might well tire of each other, but your spiritual aspirations can keep you together.

ROOSTER/DRAGON

Great affinity

Few things can come between a pairing of the Dragon and Rooster as you are secret friends of the astrological compass. You also have a connection personified by the legends that surround the celestial Dragon and Phoenix, the two ultimate creatures of the cosmic heavens that personify the ultimate Yin and Yang.

The Dragon & Rooster will always have great affinity. Your temperaments and attitudes enrich one another and whatever venture you undertake together seems always to be blessed with success.

As a couple who believe in the mutual admiration society, you build each other up very effectively indeed. You do not just depend on each other; the two of you indulge in so much ego stroking, you succeed in creating your own inner world of inspiration and aspirations. This happily, brings out the best in both of you, in a way that few can beat !

As a pair, you personify the synergy of two complementary and opposite sides of the coin coming together, and since you are both clever enough to see the advantages of your union, there is wonderful and healthy respect between the two of you. This establishes a very good basis for a successful and happy match. If you have only just met, our advice is for you to hang on close to each other. Don't let go!

But do not expect that this is a particularly loving or romantic relationship. You are simply too down to earth and practical to be go in for valentine's day cards and flowers at every anniversary! The Rooster is a clever and ambitious individual, able to see all that is valuable and productive in the headstrong but very capable and tough Dragon. In 2014 however, the Rooster's is weak while the Dragon's strength and confidence levels are formidable. This year the celestial bird leans on its cosmic mate the Dragon.

This will be **a very positive pairing** of two very action-oriented individuals but it is important not to get carried away. Play safe and play smart and you can make your cosmic yin-yang forces work very much in your favour.

Remember that the Dragon's element of Earth continually enhances Rooster's element of Metal. In 2014, it is the Dragon that will make this relationship stay strong.

ROOSTER/SNAKE

A pairing made in heaven!

The Snake and Rooster are natural soulmates of the Zodiac, being part of the trinity of intellectuals. The powerful Rooster, boosted by the *Star of Heaven*, which effectively controls the *Star of Reducing Energy* brought by the 24 Mountains, puts Rooster in a good place to pursue some great new pathways to success. Like the Snake's element pattern for the year, the Rooster has very low levels of life force and Spiritual Essence; but like the Snake, the Rooster enjoys a strong Wind Horse. Success thus comes easily to both and in 2014 it will be great success!

It will be the pursuit of success that touches a chord between the both of you this year, making you think along the same lines, bonding you seamlessly together and enabling you to fly very high indeed!

In 2014 you are excellent with each other. Both benefit the other so this is a year when Rooster and Snake will bond very closely. You will simply adore each other and the attraction goes really deep. In this relationship, the Snake is the planner, the strategist and the one with the eye for the main chance. But it is the Rooster who brings the tenacity, the decisiveness and the skills to take productive action. In 2014, the Rooster will take the lead in the relationship.

This is not surprising considering that the Rooster benefits from the *Ho Tu* of 1/6 which brings powerful wisdom to the Rooster and imbues its actions with an inner power. The Rooster enjoys this combination as a cardinal sign and does not have to share it with another sign. The Ho Tu here combines the number of the year with the number of the Period of 8 and thus is very strong For the Snake then, getting up close with the Rooster gives it access to the luck of this Ho Tu.

Together, you will surely make a powerful, unstoppable pair. The Rooster will listen to and admire the Snake's ingenious schemes and carefully thought out plans, and then put the famous Rooster efficiency to work, **transforming grand plans into reality**.

Both individuals have formidable intellects, and while the Snake is a thinker, the Rooster is practical. In business, they are hard to beat. In love, they stay devoted and true to each other, always loyal and always friends. A very passionate pair indeed and 2014 will be good for them to be together.

ROOSTER/HORSE

Empowering one another in 2014

The Horse and Rooster are not necessarily the best-matched pair. You are not naturally simpatico as one is a free spirit given to bouts of reckless and impulsive behaviour, while the other takes a more serious attitude towards life and living.

The Horse is a hang-loose sort of person, who loves speed and has a natural curiosity for the history and geography of the world, while the Rooster is down-to-earth, not given to impulsive acts or flights of fancy. There is very little the two of you actually have in common and thus, at a superficial level, it will appear there is little possibility of deep bonds that can take root in this relationship.

Your thought processes are not the same. There are many potential areas that can cause misunderstandings to arise. But in 2014 the two of you enjoy a deeply-felt harmony.

The winds of the year bring the two of you together in a love fest that leads to great happiness. The Horse and Rooster enjoy the good chi of auspicious white numbers 8 and 6, as a result of which you can actually empower one another. It is therefore a match that is worth pursuing from both points of view. If you make an effort to bring forth the best in this relationship, it will work.

A great deal of effort, tolerance and understanding is called for, but the Rooster's tenacity and the Horse's sense of adventure will be inspired by the year's good energy.

There is an aura surrounding the two of you that will radiate outwards, bringing out all that is easy going, likeable and diplomatic in the Horse personality. And even though the Rooster is a perfectionist and can be domineering, there is also a strong sense of responsibility and take-charge about the Rooster that appeals to the Horse.

The good chi of the year brings potent encouragement for you and it will compensate for whatever intrinsic differences may surface between you.

Your respective life force and inner spirit essence are weak this year, but this can be a good thing as it brings a softer edge to two cardinal signs with strong feng shui winds in your respective locations.

ROOSTER/SHEEP

Good humour will help this union

Here are two individuals who really take a lot from each other. The Sheep and Rooster are two signs with so much in common that you simply cannot be incompatible. You both have solid business brains, you possess the same high levels of creative skills in your thinking and you are action-oriented enough to make things work out well. Thus the Sheep and Rooster should really have plenty in common. Unfortunately, the two of you are simply too serious and you lack a sense of humour.

The two of you must learn to laugh together, at each other and with one another. When the atmosphere between you lightens up this way, it imbues the relationship with some truly happy vibrations, and against such a background, you will create a fertile field for good feelings to arise and take root. That is when you can both truly appreciate each other.

From there, respect can grow and you can see the way your minds inspire and strengthen your bonds with each other, and then there can be real happiness arising. Alas unless this occurs, you will eventually part company. The very attributes that cause attraction to spark between you could be what drives you apart. You will sap each other's energy. Yet with good humour, intimacy can grow. This is something that can happen in 2014 because your numbers this year are just so compatible.

In a Rooster /Sheep match, the Rooster will let go of its rigidity, softening its usual unswerving and dogmatic attitude, and the Sheep will respond with warmth and good humour. Should the Rooster allow its autocratic persona to dominate, the Sheep will feel being taken advantage of and turn away from what is perceived as bossiness. But in 2014, the feng shui winds of both Sheep and Rooster are positive. There will be no silly games of one-upmanship, no chilly silences and no sabotaging of each other. Good humour brings tolerance to a usually incompatible pair.

The Sheep's natural element is Earth while that of the Rooster's is Metal. Earth produces Metal. The Sheep is the one who will sustain this relationship and keep it going. The Rooster tends to be too proud to accept a situation too reliant on the Sheep, so a great deal of tact and diplomacy on the part of the Sheep is needed for this relationship to sustain and grow. But the ultimate result is worth it. Long term, the Sheep and Rooster bring out greatness in each other.

ROOSTER/MONKEY

Blissful at first but you may tire of each other

The Monkey and Rooster benefit from the feng shui indications of 2014 and both should enjoy good harmony and happiness this year. This is due to the chi energy that flies to your respective locations, bringing superbly compatible patterns of energies that pull you towards each other.

A Monkey who finds love with the Rooster is sure to feel a sense of bliss in the relationship, especially during the initial months. Both of you get truly enamored with each other, wanting only to spend time in one another's company.

The Rooster will be charmed by the Monkey's playfulness and cheeky asides, while the Monkey who would normally find the Rooster too old-fashioned will see great worth in the Rooster's intellectual qualities. The Monkey also regards the Rooster as having great wisdom! This is because in 2014, the Monkey and Rooster are blessed with heavenly chi that interacts magically with the *Star of Golden Deity* causing cosmic blessing energies to get generated.

The question is how long will the attraction between these two signs last?

By year's end, both sides could start finding fault. As new winds begin to blow and new energies take shape, the Monkey tires of the Rooster's obsession with logic and perfection. The Monkey is impatient at the lack of imagination of the Rooster. Equipped with an ingenious mind and a quicksilver wit, the Monkey will begin to find the Rooster's caustic cynicism tiring and discouraging. So Monkey could take off.

This will not bother the erstwhile Rooster who is put off by Monkey's perceived "irresponsible attitude". The two of you begin to realize how wide apart you are in terms of attitudes, temperaments and style. You may both be ambitious, but you differ substantially in the kind of success you each want and strive for.

The Rooster wants life's material comforts and equates success with power and prosperity, while the Monkey's aspirations have more to do with intangibles, pursuing dream projects and visions that inspire its creativity and challenges its imagination. Your motivations thus differ substantially. Those in a marriage find that while early years were promising and exciting, you are likely to have grown apart with the passing years.

ROOSTER/ROOSTER

Two self-centered individuals could find a pairing between them difficult

When two Roosters get together, the obvious synergy suggests that this could well be a great match. It might appear that you enjoy perfect understanding of one another and thus appreciate what really motivates you both. Sadly, this belief that you are so similar you are sure to be compatible cannot be further from the truth.

The reality is that the Rooster character tends to be self-centered and there is a general tendency towards arrogance. You are a very stubborn and dogmatic sign and when two Roosters get together, initial attraction and mutual admiration of each other simply gives rise to boredom and intolerance.

When two Roosters get together, the attributes that make you a synergistic pair at the start may ultimately work against you.

In 2014 however, the Rooster tends to soften their attitudes towards others. You benefit from divine energy, making you a lot easier to live with. Two Roosters can find a level of happiness and stability together as a result.

It seems you have become convinced of the beneficial effect of practising tolerance. With diplomacy entering the picture, a match between two Roosters can work.

This is because while the Rooster sign can be unyielding, made stubborn by your Metal essence, in 2014, you find that you are in fact uncharacteristically easy to deal with. There is less nagging on your part and lots more of giving in. As a result, bickering is kept to a minimum. The giant ego of the Rooster gets a lift this year!

The yin Rooster's natural element is Metal. Two Roosters together can bring too much Metal to the equation and this might harden your nature in a way that can be detrimental to both; hurting you as a couple as well as individually.

This year, the Rooster is weak due to the low reading of your life force and spirit essence. In this match, neither of you appear strong enough to take charge. The good news is that you are both blessed by the number 6, which brings auspicious heavenly energy; as a result, despite the presence of conflict energy, you are able to benefit from the 1/6 *Ho Tu*, which brings you the luck of sound common sense and good wisdom.

ROOSTER/DOG

Little understanding between this pair

The Rooster and Dog are unable to communicate with each other in 2014, and even if you can, you will be talking along parallel lines as there is little if any understanding. This year unfortunately, the Dog is bad for the Rooster, and for the sake of both signs, it is better not to pursue anything that might lead to a serious relationship. This year, the path of true love will not run smooth for the two of you.

When these two individuals first get together, they talk but do not communicate. This is because both give voice to lofty ideals but do not listen to each other.

The moral high ground is the Dog's favourite topic of conversation. He/she takes pride in the nobler instincts of Man. Virtues like honor, integrity, loyalty and honestly are important to the Dog and the attraction of the Rooster is that the Dog believes that you personify these traits.

But these high expectations merely set the Dog up for disappointment not because the Rooster is dishonest or dishonourable but because the Dog's expectations are unrealistic. The Rooster does appreciate the softer side of the Dog's personality, especially during the early stages of courtship, but this soon disappears in the face of the Dog's severely afflicted bad luck. The Dog is hit by the misfortune star *wu wang*, which turns Dog sign into an insufferable pessimist.

The Dog will get impatient with the Rooster's tendency to be indecisive this year. The Dog is supremely confident, while the Rooster is assailed by self doubt. This arise from the severe mismatch of energies between this pair.

The Dog is strong and confident this year, enjoying a powerful life force and Inner Essence – the Rooster on the other hand is weak in 2014 and does not take kindly to the mismatch of energy levels. The pragmatic side of the Rooster has little chance to assert itself as the Dog, afflicted by the *wu wang*, becomes stubborn and unyielding.

The match has difficulty working because neither side is prepared to make allowances. Both are stubborn and they view their disappointment as disillusionment. One blames the other for all the shortcomings of the match. This lack of understanding between the two of makes it better for you to split.

ROOSTER/BOAR

Bringing out the best in each other

The domineering and aggressive Rooster can find love and comfort in the arms of the easy-going and affable Boar, who despite it being a difficult year is still able to look on the bright side of things. As a result, the Rooster's interests gets piqued.

The Boar's seemingly disorganized and undisciplined approach to life brings out the Rooster's natural protective take-charge instincts.

Funnily enough, the Boar is also feeling protective of the Rooster, as a result of which both sides can find comfort with one another. The Boar is able to tolerate the Rooster's moodiness through the year. Indeed 2014 is a potpourri of good and bad luck for the Rooster, while for the Boar it is misfortune and conflict all the way.

The two signs can be totally taken up coping with each other's respective energy afflictions. The year does not exactly help this pair, with energy patterns that could well bring too many challenges and obstacles. Discussion between the Rooster and Boar will be mostly one-sided, although surprisingly, quarrels between the two of you rarely lead to excessive controversy or fist fights. The Boar is not the fighting type and prefers to walk away at the first signs of trouble.

But the Boar knows how to handle the Rooster, and vice versa as a result of which there are unexpected flashes of brilliance in this match. They bring out the best in each other. Spurred on by the Boar's quiet encouragement, and helped along by his/her mate's admirable networking skills, the Rooster will have much to crow about in terms of career and business accomplishments. This is a good match indeed. Both parties can look forward to a happy time together.

The Rooster's natural element is Metal. That of the Boar is Water. In the cycle of element relationships, Metal produces Water, which in this case indicates that the Rooster will be the partner giving support in this match. It is likely that Rooster will be the breadwinner of the family. And because the Rooster is protective and responsible, this relationship might work out in the long run.

The Boar is generally appreciative of the Rooster.

THE 6 DIFFERENT HOUSE PAIRINGS

ZODIAC HOUSE	ANIMALS	YIN/YANG	SKILLS UNLEASHED
HOUSE OF CREATIVITY & CLEVERNESS	RAT	YANG	The Rat initiates
	OX	YIN	The Ox completes
HOUSE OF GROWTH & DEVELOPMENT	TIGER	YANG	The Tiger employs force
	RABBIT	YIN	The Rabbit uses diplomacy
HOUSE OF MAGIC & SPIRITUALITY	DRAGON	YANG	The Dragon creates magic
	SNAKE	YIN	The Snake creates mystery
HOUSE OF PASSION & SEXUALITY	HORSE	YANG	The Horse embodies male energy
	SHEEP	YIN	The Sheep is the female energy
HOUSE OF CAREER & COMMERCE	MONKEY	YANG	The Monkey creates strategy
	ROOSTER	YIN	The Rooster gets things moving
HOUSE OF DOMESTICITY	DOG	YANG	The Dog works to provide
	BOAR	YIN	The Boar enjoys what is created

PART FIVE
ROOSTER'S PERSONAL FENG SHUI IN 2014

WEST 2: the ROOSTER'S HOME LOCATION
Subduing afflictive stars affecting you in 2014

ENHANCING THE WEST TO IMPROVE ROOSTER'S LUCK
Activating the Heavenly Star 6 in the WEST

THE DZAMBHALA RITUAL FOR WEALTH
Inviting Dzambhala & the four prosperity dakinis into your home

THE POWER "ELEPHANT" FOR EVERYTHING AUSPICIOUS
The elephant with its amulet wheel transforms the home

DOUBLE DORJE SYMBOL TO SUBDUE DISASTERS
Lends cosmic authority and protects against being a victim

YIN WATER REMEDY TO SUBDUE ILL WINDS
The five element YIN WATER remedy

West: the Rooster's Home Location

Subduing afflictive stars affecting you in 2014

The Rooster direction in the compass is described as the *yu* direction and it is one of the 24 mountain directions in the feng shui *luo pan*. This direction corresponds to the exact West 2 direction on the compass and occupies fifteen degrees from 262.5 degrees to 277.5 degrees.

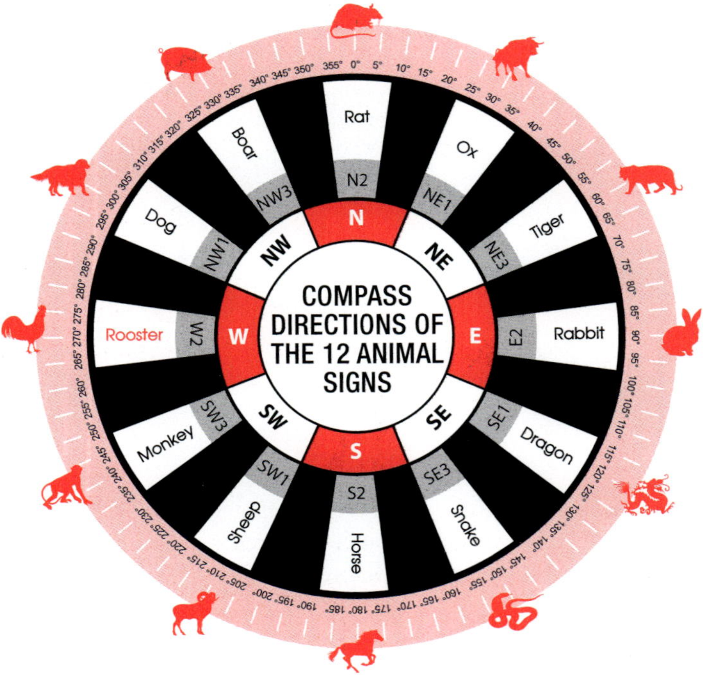

If you want to enjoy good feng shui luck through the year, familiarize yourself with where **West** is in your home and office, and then make sure you follow the suggestions given here to protect and enhance your luck. The first thing demanding your attention each new year is to be aware of all the afflictions that can cause harmful chi to accumulate in your home location of West.

Check that the West sector of your important rooms and of your home are not blocked by old magazines, newspapers or carelessly discarded items. The build-up of junk occurs in every home and office. It is advisable to consciously clear clutter from your sign's home direction. Anything that appears untidy and seeming to block the flow of chi in your location will block your luck.

Corners that are cluttered cause yin chi to build up, and if the sector that is blocked is your auspicious location or your home location, your feng shui luck will suffer.

A golden rule of feng shui is that chi energy must flow smoothly unimpeded through the home and through **your animal sign home location**. Blockages of any kind caused by furniture that sticks out or dead plants or junk, can cause different aspects of your life to get stalled. Definitely success will get blocked. Unexpected difficulties manifest! It benefits you to take the trouble to spring clean your home and office once a year.

Sector Affinity

Note that the Rooster's exact home location is the 15 degrees corresponding to the subsector West 2, and you are not sharing this sector with any other sign. The entire West sector is deemed to be your home location because you are a cardinal direction sign; you need not share the sector with another sign.

When lucky stars fly to the West, the Rooster can keep all the good fortune to itself. Likewise, when affliction stars fly to the West, you bear the brunt of the bad luck all by yourself and there is no other sign to help dilute the negative effects of whatever afflictive star is brought by the year's feng shui winds! In 2014, the entire 45 degrees of West is home to the heavenly white star 6, which brings unexpected good fortune.

This is considered an auspicious indication and the number 6 being a white number is regarded as one of the three most auspicious stars of the feng shui chart. The star of 6 will benefit the Rooster in several ways, mostly related to unexpected hidden support and cosmic patronage. The West is the place on the compass that points to descendents luck, so your children are sure to benefit from the heavenly 6 star. In younger households, this star can bring a new addition to the family if your bedroom is located in the West sector of your home.

Subduing Afflictive Stars That Affect You in 2014

In 2014, the Rooster benefits from good feng shui winds bringing an auspicious star number. There are no afflictions brought by the feng shui chart of 2014. But you do need to take care of the annual conflict stars flanking your home location. Note the afflictions are indirect, so they bring minor problems that can be subdued with feng shui placement cures.

CONFLICT STARS: In the 24 Mountains chart, your home location of West 2 is next to yearly conflict stars, on your right (in W1) and on your left (W3). These conflict stars need to be pacified by placing Fire energy in the form of a **bright light** or having **something red** placed on either side of the West 2 sector of any room and also the W2 sector of the whole house.

Should your West sector be too dark, or the windows here block out the sunlight caused by trees that have grown too tall and thick with leaves, it can cause conflict chi to actualize in quarrels and misunderstandings. When there is too much shade in the West sector of your garden and around the house, you must do something to increase the sunlight, as this will strengthen the Fire energy of the sector. This is what you need to counter the effect of the conflict stars near your home location.

The Rooster should also be aware of the *Reducing Energy Star* that flies to your home location. Coupled with the fact that your life force is weak, this means that you should be extra careful about overexerting yourself this year. Take it easy, and in the West sector place **crystals** to strengthen Earth element. This keeps your intrinsic energy of Metal strong!

On your body, it is beneficial to wear the **Tortoise Chakra amulet pendant** to strengthen your personal Metal energy. The Rooster benefits from this chakra amulet in 2014.

Enhancing Auspicious Stars That Bring Good Fortune in 2014

In 2014, the Rooster benefits from one lucky indication, brought by the Flying Star number 6, which flies into the West, your home location.

This will have a very beneficial input on the Rooster's fortunes in 2014, as it indicates heaven's blessings. This star number brings you the luck of mentors and the patronage of influential people. The star of 6 puts you in the good graces of the powerful people in your life such as your boss, your important clients and your customers. It also brings you the luck of the heavenly nobleman.

To benefit from the star of 6, which some regard as the **Star of the Qui Ren**, i.e. the helpful nobleman who signifies the supportive person in your life who will give you your chance to make it big, we highly recommend that you activate this beneficial indication. Place a powerful **image of God of Heaven** or decorate this sector with the **seven royal emblems** which include the potent presence of the powerful minister and the courageous general. You can also have the **Jade Emperor holding a sun and moon windchime** here to actualize help from influential and powerful people in your life.

Toilets, Store Rooms & Kitchens

At the same time please ensure that the energy of West is not in any way afflicted by the presence of an open toilet or a closed storeroom in this part of your home. This can cause bad feng shui for the Rooster, bringing obstacles to your professional and work life.

A **toilet** in the Rooster corner can be the cause of problems developing at the office. Note that your success luck will definitely be adversely affected if there is a toilet located in your compass location. It is sure to clash with your personal Wind Horse, affecting its strength and vigour. The toilet here will create obstacles to success luck and hurt your work environment. It is worth considering relocating the toilet; or at least reduce its use.

Meanwhile, if there is a **store room** in your Rooster location of West, it can cause your auspicious heavenly mentor luck of 2014 to get locked up. As a result, your expectations will be hard to actualize and you will be overcome with self-doubt, which affects your level of confidence. Your ability to think clearly is certain to be affected resulting in the possibility of hasty and unwise decisions. Here the best remedy is to remove the store room altogether by knocking down the walls. If you cannot do this, at least clear out the junk; install a bright light and give the room a fresh coat of white paint.

If the **kitchen** occupies the Rooster location in the home, it causes a particularly harmful aspect. The kitchen signifies Fire energy, which is harmful to Rooster's Metal element. However, note that Fire energy in West 1 and West 3 is good, as it exhausts the negative effect of the annual conflict stars brought by the 24 Mountains here.

Displaying the Power Elephant

An excellent symbolic placement that can increase the Rooster's luck in 2014 is to place the **Power Elephant with Amulet Wheel** in the West corner of your work desk. Images of elephants always attract very strongly positive luck.

Elephants are regarded as celestial creatures still living in the world as many others are already extinct and survive only in our minds via their forms still being crafted and placed as house guardians. The elephant is not extinct. It still exists and thus, is not regarded as a celestial creature. From a spiritual feng shui perspective, however, this worldly creature can channel celestial abundance into your world.

The elephant has always had a sacred ambience as it is believed that Buddha was an elephant in a past life, and before his birth, Buddha's mother dreamt of a white elephant entering into her body; hence it is a creature revered by Buddhists.

Many believe the Power Elephant with Amulet Wheel, when placed in the home, can channel big abundance from the cosmos.

So if you are working on closing a deal, pitching for a project or angling for a particular job, display one on your desk or on a table in the Southwest of your home or office. It will add strength to your authority. People will respect you and what you say a great deal more.

Feng Shui of the Rooster at Work

The year 2014 is definitely a year of success for the Rooster, although you do have to cope with bouts of low energy. You will also feel a low level of confidence, but there is hidden support from unexpected benefactors.

However, whether or not you can successfully actualize exciting and positive new developments on the career and business front depends on how successful you are at strengthening your own inner determination and your belief in your own capabilities.

FENG SHUI TIP: Placing the **Power Elephant** near you at work helps enormously because the Rooster sign needs additional power chi to help you cut through self-doubt.

Your spiritual and physical strength are at low levels, so it is understandable that many of you will lack the will to take risks or stray from the familiar. You have the luck to succeed but you lack inner zeal. The truth is that you find it hard to get excited about anything really and the problem is that you lack the inspiration. If you can get into the warrior spirit and enhance your personal willpower, the year will seem far more exciting. When you can positively psyche yourself into a state of inner enthusiasm, you will be much better inspired to create exciting prospects for yourself. From a feng shui perspective the outlook is actually very encouraging, so you should not fear striking out in a new direction, making a strategic change and even forging a powerful new alliance.

You only need to believe in yourself and give yourself a chance to fly; let your powerful *lung ta* take wing. This way even though your life force and spirit essence are at weak levels, you can systematically strengthen all your relevant elements to take full advantage of your excellent number 6 star in the feng shui flying star chart! In terms of cosmic energy, the Rooster is in a position to create your own good luck.

Feng Shui of the Rooster's Health

All indications taken together suggest that the Rooster needs to consciously guard against getting sick. Your life force and Spiritual Essence are weak and you will be more susceptible than other signs to succumbing to illness. It is important to make sure you do not sleep in a bedroom located in the East, as the illness star is located there in 2014.

The **21 year old Water Rooster** and **33 year old Metal Rooster** are two Rooster signs with a low health reading, so the two of you could experience problematic health scares this year. For you both, it is advisable to preempt the situation with the powerful cosmic cures. Place a **golden wu lou** by your bedside to keep sickness chi away from your bedroom.

We recommend that should the **Water or Metal Rooster** get sick this year, to wear **dark blue and earth colours** respectively. These reflect the use of element therapy to strengthen your health luck.

It is advisable to wear the **Medicine Buddha watch** through the year! This has the moving mantra and the image of the healing Buddha. It is incredibly effective at keeping you much less susceptible to illness chi and if you do fall ill, Medicine Buddha will help you recover fast.

The **33 year old Metal Rooster** benefits from wearing a **gemstone** that is **yellow in colour.** Thus citrines are ideal for helping you stay well through the year. Gemstones are usually excellent for guarding against serious illness. The type of gemstone to wear is usually associated with the planets under the Indian Astrology system or investigating the element you need for a specific purpose.

Fire and Wood Rooster are the signs that enjoy robust good health through the year and need not do anything special.

The Rooster's Lucky Directions

Using your lucky directions based on Eight Mansions feng shui is an easy way to capture good luck, but auspicious directions do get afflicted by the energies of each new year. Unlucky directions likewise can also be influenced by good stars that bring good fortune. It is beneficial to stay up to date on your facing and sitting directions.

Lucky and unlucky directions are divided into East and West directions.

EAST directions are East, SE, North and South
WEST directions are West, NW, SW and NE.

Depending on whether you are an East or West person, one set of directions is beneficial and the other non-beneficial for you. There are East and West people, likewise East and West houses, rooms, corners and so forth. In feng shui, everything is categorised according to whether it is East or West.

WEST people always do better and are happier when using West directions, spaces and locations. For them, all East directions and locations are unlucky. EAST group people benefit from East directions and locations in the same way and are hurt by West directions which bring them bad luck. All directions are affected by the changing energies of every new year. Knowing how your lucky directions are affected is part of the feng shui updating process.

When you sit facing a direction that is auspicious for you, it always brings you luck; it is the best way of instantly improving your feng shui. Try it when you are hoping to land a job, close a deal, ask for a favour or impress someone.

You will be amazed by how easy it is to activate good fortune simply by using your personal lucky directions and avoiding your inauspicious directions.

The Rooster in 2014 is going through a year when you will need to stay mentally strong and positive to maintain yourself at the top of situations and to have the capability to transform opportunities into success. You should definitely use feng shui to ensure that your success luck is not harmed in any way by inadvertently sitting or facing a direction that is either bad for you or is afflicted this year.

This is based on a method of compass feng shui which focuses on tapping into one's auspicious facing and sitting directions. It is one of the best ways of attracting strong and healthy good luck and is part of the feng shui that is used so successfully in Taiwan and China today. The right direction brings added hidden energies that are helpful to you based on your year of birth and your gender. Thus the table of good luck directions are different for men and women.

Facing your success or self-development directions strengthens success and growth luck for yourself in your professional and work life. It benefits you by increasing your sense of abundance and it helps you to grow in stature and prosperity. It brings the luck of increase!

Male Roosters who belong to the WEST group have Northwest as their success direction and this is a badly afflicted direction in 2014). West group men have West as their personal growth directions and this is very auspicious. This is the best direction to face in 2014.

The **69 year old** and **33 year old men Roosters** belong to the EAST group and these two Roosters have Southeast as their *sheng chi* direction, which is an afflicted direction. The star number of the SE sector in 2014 is the hostility and misunderstanding star of 3.

The **45 year old Earth Rooster** however who has North as their *sheng chi* direction can face North, as it has the lucky star of 9 there. You can also face South as the auspicious star of 8 has flown to the South. But do note that South 2 hosts the Tai Sui this year, so facing South 2 is not advisable. Men Roosters whose *sheng chi* direction is afflicted in 2014 should look for another auspicious direction to face that is not afflicted by the feng shui winds of the year.

For Rooster women, all of you belong to the WEST group; your *sheng chi* or success direction is either Southwest or Northeast depending on your heavenly stem element. Note here that Northeast is afflicted with the number 7 star in 2014. You should avoid facing either Northeast in 2014 even if this direction is good for you.

The best directions for WEST group people this year are West or Southwest.

These are the two directions to face when working or speaking with someone important. For 2014, the same guidelines apply to all Rooster women as well as to men who belong to the West group. The direction for all of you to strenuously avoid is Northwest, a direction that is afflicted by the misfortune *five yellow* star.

AUSPICIOUS DIRECTIONS FOR ROOSTER MEN

YEAR OF BIRTH/AGE	HS ELEMENT	SUCCESS DIRECTION	HEALTH DIRECTION	LOVE DIRECTION	PERSONAL GROWTH DIRECTION
1945/69 YEARS	Wood Rooster	SE *333*	East *222*	South ***	North
1957/57 YEARS	Fire Rooster	NW *555*	SW	NE *777*	West
1969/45 YEARS	Earth Rooster	North	South ***	East *222*	SE *333*
1981/33 YEARS	Metal Rooster	SE *333*	East *222*	South ***	North
1993/21 YEARS	Water Rooster	NW *555*	SW	NE *777*	West
2005/9 YEARS	Wood Rooster	North	South ***	East *222*	SE *333*

The following afflicted directions must be noted for 2014.

222 - Shows illness afflicted direction in 2014

777 - Afflicted by the Violence & Betrayal Star

333 - Afflicted by the Quarrelsome Star 3

555 - Afflicted by the Wu Wang 5 Yellow

*** - Direction is enjoying excellent feng shui luck in 2014

AUSPICIOUS DIRECTIONS FOR ROOSTER WOMEN

YEAR OF BIRTH/AGE	HS ELEMENT	SUCCESS DIRECTION	HEALTH DIRECTION	LOVE DIRECTION	PERSONAL GROWTH DIRECTION
1945/69 YEARS	Wood Rooster	SW	NW *555*	West	NE *777*
1957/57 YEARS	Fire Rooster	SW	NW *555*	West	NE *777*
1969/45 YEARS	Earth Rooster	NE *777*	West	NW *555*	SW
1981/33 YEARS	Metal Rooster	SW	NW *555*	West	NE *777*
1993/21 YEARS	Water Rooster	SW	NW *555*	West	NE *777*
2005/9 YEARS	Wood Rooster	NE *777*	West	NW *555*	SW

The following afflicted directions must be noted for 2014.

222 - Shows illness afflicted direction in 2014

777 - Afflicted by the Violence & Betrayal Star

333 - Afflicted by the Quarrelsome Star 3

555 - Afflicted by the Wu Wang 5 Yellow

*** - Direction is enjoying excellent feng shui luck in 2014

Check the preceding tables, which reveal all the four good directions of those born in the years of the Rooster. For those of you belonging to the WEST group do take note that for you, the direction West is your Group's most auspicious direction as it plays host to the heavenly star of 6 which goes on to create a Ho Tu combination of 1/6 – both of these are lucky indications so for you all, facing West brings great good fortune.

For those of you who cannot face West, you can also choose to face Southwest, as this is another lucky direction bringing the luck of victory. You can use this direction to activate your professional luck and for some of you it also benefits your romance luck.

The **Southwest** direction is associated with the luck of marriage, and those who are single and looking for marriage partners can sleep in bedrooms in this sector to improve their love life. Those already married this direction can improve your chances of trying for a new baby.

Note that for East group Rooster men, South is the most auspicious direction as this brings the luck of the number 8 as long as you do not face South 2. The East is afflicted by the number 2 illness star. The Southeast is also unlucky as the hostile 3 is here but North is acceptable and may even be lucky for some of you.

Avoid facing any one of your four unlucky directions i.e. all the East group directions if you are a WEST group person, and West directions if you an EAST person. Thus take note:

WEST PEOPLE, please avoid facing all East group directions and also the following directions even though they may be lucky for you:

- **NORTHWEST** because facing this direction can cause you to become a victim of the *wu wang*, which brings illness, loss and accidents. This is an aggravating star, although in 2014 it is not at its strongest. Nevertheless, do be careful if you work in this sector. Facing NW can be acceptable as long as you are not too noisy. But place the **5 Yellow remedy** here before you do so.

  For all of you Rooster men, irrespective of whether you are East or West group, please be very careful of this NW direction as it signifies the Patriarch. Facing NW can cause the man of the family and all men in leadership positions to suffer setbacks and misfortune.

- **NORTHEAST** because this is where the violent star 7 resides, bringing risk of armed robbery affecting your household. It is strong in 2014, so avoid activating it by choosing not to work in this sector. Facing it is fine, as long as you are wearing the **Water colours** of black or blue and the **remedy against the 7** has been put into place.

EAST PEOPLE should not face any of the West group directions and also avoid directly facing these lucky directions of yours:

- **SOUTHEAST** because facing OR disturbing this direction activates the number 3 quarrelsome star, which causes loss, cause you to get involved in litigation due to hostility and misunderstandings. It can also cause your household to become a victim of injustice or scams. The number 3 star is very strong this year, but it is easy to suppress. Use the **9 Amulets cure**.

- **EAST** because this direction is afflicted by illness winds. This is not a strong affliction in 2014 and remedies will work efficiently when placed correctly – the best are the **wu lou windchimes.** But it is nevertheless advisable to avoid activating this direction by facing it.

Capture Good Directions

Having determined your personal lucky directions, you can improve your feng shui in 2014 by using your lucky directions while you sleep, eat and work. Adjust your furniture to let you capture a lucky direction that is not afflicted.

Do this as early in the year as possible. It is worth the effort as the direction you sleep, eat or work with really does make a difference to your luck and wellbeing. It is not just about success or wealth; it is about creating wellness and staying safe and healthy. There are different ways to use lucky directions in the home. The challenge is to do so without getting harmed by secret poison arrows, such as sitting under a beam or facing a pointed edge of a pillar.

Take note of the following for 2014:

- **Rearrange your bed so your head is pointed to a lucky direction.** For those belonging to the WEST group, **Southwest and West are favourable** and not afflicted in 2014. For those belonging to the EAST group, the South is favoured, but only for sleeping. But the **North** is also a good sleeping direction.

- **Rearrange your sitting direction at the dining table and at the work desk.** Follow the same guideline except EAST group should really only **face North**, as facing South makes you confront the *Tai Sui,* which brings harmful luck.

Also take note that if you are sleeping in the corner that corresponds to your home direction (for the Rooster it is West 2) you will enjoy a comfortable sleep each night. Usually you can also "borrow' the luck of your astrological allies by tapping into their good luck directions; although in 2014 note that the Ox and Snake directions are both afflicted.

Meanwhile, note also that while the Rooster can also tap into the Dragon's direction of SE3, unfortunately it too is afflicted this year. **The best for the Rooster is to face your own home direction.**

Avoid sleeping in the corner that is directly opposite your Rooster home direction i.e. East 2, since this is astrologically, your hostile corner. You also run the risk of unnecessarily confronting your astrological enemy, the Rabbit, who resides in the East 2 location. In any case, the East is an afflicted direction in 2014.

Increasing Wealth Luck in 2014

Each year, your personal wealth luck changes due to the interaction of your own wealth element with that of the year. This year, the element of wealth under the system of element calculation is WOOD. To enhance your personal wealth luck you need to know how your own wealth element at birth interacts with WOOD. (This is summarised in the chart below.)

ENHANCING WEALTH LUCK WITH THE ELEMENTS

HEAVENLY STEM /AGE IN 2014	YOUR WEALTH ELEMENT	Quality of Wealth Luck in 2014 & How to Enhance your Wealth Luck i.e. strengthen it this year
WOOD ROOSTER/ 69 YEARS	WOOD	X - bad. Increase WATER energy around you.
FIRE ROOSTER/ 57 YEARS	FIRE	OOO - excellent. No need to do anything!
EARTH ROOSTER/ 45 YEARS	EARTH	XX - very bad. Strengthen FIRE energy near you.
METAL ROOSTER/ 33 YEARS	METAL	OO - very good. Increase EARTH energy around you.
WATER ROOSTER/ 21 YEARS	WATER	OX - neutral. Increase METAL Energy around you.

You can strengthen your personal Wealth Luck by increasing the element that produces your own wealth element as summarised in the chart above. For the **57 year old Fire Rooster,** there is no need to increase Wood energy as you already have it brought to you by the year's wealth element.

INCREASING FIRE ENERGY means adding **bright lights** around you. Note that yellow golden light is better than white fluorescent lights.

INCREASING EARTH ENERGY means surrounding your immediate environment with auspicious symbols made of stone/earth/crystals such as **porcelain vases, crystal balls** and so forth.

INCREASING METAL ENERGY means hanging **metal windchimes** that create the sound of metal near you. Choose auspicious wind chimes that emit pleasing sounds. This will strengthen the Water, your wealth element. Please note that the chimes must be all-metal, as this is an element enhancer.

INCREASING WATER ENERGY means placing **water features** near you. Here the water should be moving to generate live "yang" water. An aquarium or **small zen fountain** will do very nicely.

Display the **White Dzambhala Plaque** prominently in your home. This beautiful plaque contains the image of Dzambhala with his four goodesses and their mantras to generate swift blessings of financial stability and wealth in your home. If you wish, you can perform the daily bathing ritual on these five wealth deities to attract wealth luck into your home.

Special Wealth Ritual

Place the five deity images on a stand inside a large decorative bowl, and while reciting the mantras of the four deities, **pour water very slowly** over the head and body of the Dzambhala and four wealth offering Goddesses.

The mantra of the Dzambhala:
OM PADMA KRODA AYAH DZAMBHALA SHRI DHAYA HUM PEH

The mantra of the four offering goddesses:
- OM VAJRA DAKINI HUM PEH
- OM RATNA DAKINI HUM PEH
- OM PADMA DAKINI HUM PEH
- OM KARMA DAKINI HUM PEH / SARVA SIDDHI HUM

Recite each of the mantras 21 times then use the leftover water to bathe! Do not throw the water away. You can also boil it to make tea but bathing in Dzambhala water is the BEST way to receive the wealth blessings of these powerful deities.

You can also look for the special **Dzambhala Fountain** and place all five deities on the fountain. Place this feature in your own Southwest location and this will also activate the *indirect spirit* of the current period of 8 which brings wealth luck.

Note that to benefit from wealth luck, you need to be physically and spiritually strong. Your life force and Spirit essence must be robust. The Monkey is weak this year, so it is more difficult for you to actualize wealth luck unless you strengthen your life force and spirit essence using element therapy. Note that you always need to have a good personal level of yang chi that brings strong vitality for you to enjoy good fortune.

Good fortune can also get blocked when the cosmic spirits around you feel neglected. Usually to ensure they do not bring obstacles your way, you can use incense offering ritual with mantra recitation to placate the spirit beings who occupy your home with you. This way you add the all important dimension of spiritual feng shui to make the year go smoothly for you in terms of enjoying more money and income luck.

Double Dorje symbol to Subdue Disaster Indication

Lends cosmic authority & protects against being a victim

In 2014, the 24 Mountains bring a great many conflict stars. The Rooster has to contend with two yearly conflict stars, which are on either side of your home location of West 2. These conflict stars combine with the Horse Year's aggressive swords to make it a year when anger energy and tension simmers beneath the surface. Everyone including you MUST subdue aggressive behavior and ensure that tempers do not flare into violence.

A good way to stay on top of any angry situation is to display the **Double Dorje** also known as the double vajra. The word "vajra" means thunderbolt. This can be looked on as a subduing implement which signifies authority over the forces of evil nagas that bring mental afflictions, violence and disturbances to worldly human realms. This is a spiritual feng shui remedy that exudes protective vibrations into the space it occupies or around the aura of the person wearing it. It works as a formidable talisman generated by its shape and form!

The Double Dorje exudes protective and positive vibrations into the space it occupies.

This is also a tantric tool used by yogics; indeed the double dorje has many secret powers associated with powerful meditations done at deeper spiritual levels. The vibrations it generates are invisible and for us, it is sufficient to use or wear it, display or place it inside the home to benefit from its cosmic significance.

The other benefit of displaying the Double Dorje in the home is that its presence is always felt by the local spirit landlords of your space; cosmic beings instantly recognize its power. Having this symbol in the home will make everything move a lot more smoothly for you and your household.

There is less danger of residents falling victim to 'spirit harm' which manifests in different ways. Often it brings a sudden illness usually to a young child. But this is almost always followed by a sudden change of mood. A child or teenager, previously happy and enthusiastic turning belligerent or moody, or worse, losing interest in school or in friends.

If someone in your household is suffering from acute depression or is exhibiting strange behaviour, it is always beneficial to enlist the help of your local spirit landlords by making incense or "sur" offerings of three sweets and three whites, which we described in our books last year. Usually a mild attack of spirit harm can be overcome by appealing to your guardian spirit landlords, especially if you have been making **regular incense offerings.**

But having the Double Dorje symbol in the home adds to the home's protection against spirit harm. Place it on a side cabinet either in the living area or in the dining room. If you already have the **three suns** and **two moon mirrors**, place the Double Dorje next to these other powerful cures that enlist the auric glow of the sun and moon.

These are spiritual remedies that add vigourous cosmic brilliance to your home. They are small, beautiful, inexpensive and extremely effective in ensuring your life through this year of the ferocious Horse is smooth and untroubled - like ensuring an oasis of calm amidst some seriously fierce winds of conflict raging around the world!

Yin Water to Subdue Ill Winds

Also known as the five-element YIN WATER remedy

In 2014, which is a Yang year, the 5 Element **Yin Water Cure** containing stone symbols of the five elements goes a long way towards calming the fiery turbulence of the Horse Year. We have already noted the two stars of *Aggressive Swords,* which bring the danger of serious conflicts escalating into severe violence scenarios that include bloodshed... so at our micro domestic levels of existence, it really is beneficial to install this Yin Water remedy in the home.

The world seems to have become a more dangerous place and from a feng shui perspective, we believe that prevention is always the best strategy; hence we are recommending all homes to put this easy remedy in place. Have it near the front of the house if possible within sight of the main door.

For the Rooster, place this in the West.

Take five small glass containers, fill them with water and place coloured stones inside according to the following:

- Use **black stones** to signify the **Water element**. In 2014, this element is missing from the year's chart. It represents **power, recognition and authority**. Without Water, your voice cannot be heard. Your speech lacks power.

- Use **yellow stones** to signify the **Earth element**. In 2014, this element is missing from the chart and it is an important element because there is so much Fire energy. Earth keeps Fire under control, exhausting its fiery nature while using its brilliance.

- The Earth element stands for **creativity, cleverness and intelligence.** It is the binding force that harnesses everything else. Its presence in the Yin Water remedy ensures that thinking minds override potential violence and temper tantrums that can put household members in danger.

- Use **white stones** to signify the **Metal element**. In 2014, this is the element that represents **wealth, prosperity and business success.** It is the enhancing agent that can increase your sales, expand your order books and enlarge your channels of distribution. There is only one Metal in the year's chart.

- Use **green stones** to represent **Wood element**. This is the resource element, which ensures the year is not short of the resources needed to keep prosperity chi moving. In 2014, there is no shortage of this element, but Wood is the only element that brings growth. This makes Wood a vital part of the living process. But there is no need to add to the year's supply. The Wood element does however taper off towards the end of the year.

- Use **red stones** to signify **Fire element**. In 2014, the year is awash with Fire energy. Indeed some would say there is too much Fire! Everything associated with this fast-rising element that also burns out just as quickly, has to do with effort, drive, ambition and an inner competitive spirit that can very easily get out of hand!

  The Fire energy represented in the Yin Water remedy is excellent, because the red stones are submerged under water, bringing in the cooling effects of water. This will keep brilliant Fire under control and helps prevent the rise of the three poisons associated with competitiveness - anger, jealousy and violence.

PART SIX

FLYING STAR HO TU COMBINATIONS

The Rooster directly benefits from the Ho Tu of 1 & 6

The Rooster benefits directly from one of the Ho Tu combinations that appear in 2014's Flying Star Feng Shui chart. However, in addition, because there is a complete set of auspicious Ho Tu combinations making an appearance in the year's chart, and with them all in their waxing cycle, there is also a special aura of cosmic good fortune that pervades the year. The Rooster can benefit from the Ho Tu combinations by energizing the compass locations where they occur.

But first, **what is the HO TU combination** and why is it so auspicious?

The Ho Tu is part of the Flying Star compass formula used extensively by practicing masters in Hong Kong, Taiwan and China. Flying Star has become the most popular of the time dimension formulas and it is hi by overseas Chinese, mainly because it is not difficult to apply in the context of modern living and also because it offers a very accurate way of deciphering the changing energy patterns that affect the luck of buildings from year to year and from period to period.

The key to successfully using Flying Star is in the interpretation of the nine numbers & the way these combine to reveal lucky and unlucky indications for a variety of human aspirations – luck in work, business, health, wealth & marriage.

Each of the single numbers from 1 to 9 symbolizes a certain kind of luck with nuances of its manifestation that vary from year to year depending on a variety of factors. But more revealing is when each of the numbers combines with another in a lucky way within a specific compass sector. Such combinations often indicate quite extraordinary luck for those who know how to activate and make the most of them.

One of the most powerfully lucky of combinations is that of the Ho Tu, which is said to have been brought on the back of the **Dragon Horse**.

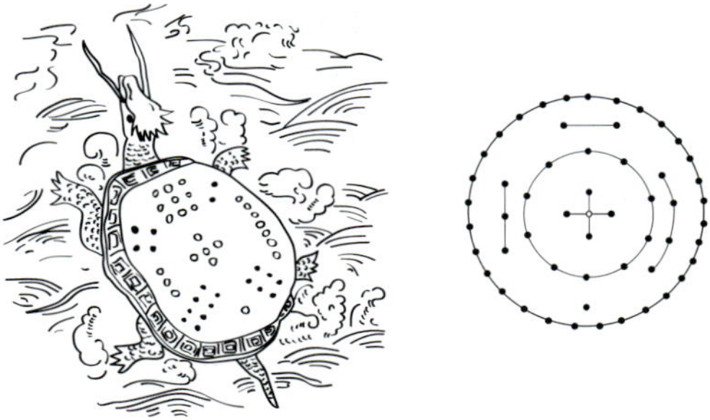

The Lo Shu numbers brought by the Tortoise

The Ho Tu Combination of numbers brought by the Dragon Horse

According to Feng Shui legend, the Ho Tu combinations were an extension of the Lo Shu pattern of numbers brought by the Tortoise emerging from the River Lo that was discovered by *Fu Hsi*, who is generally regarded as the founder of all things esoteric in Chinese history. And as all those familiar with feng shui will know, the Lo Shu is the magic square of nine numbered grids that is the basis of the Flying Star formula.

THE HO TU SQUARE & ITS NUMBER COMBINATIONS

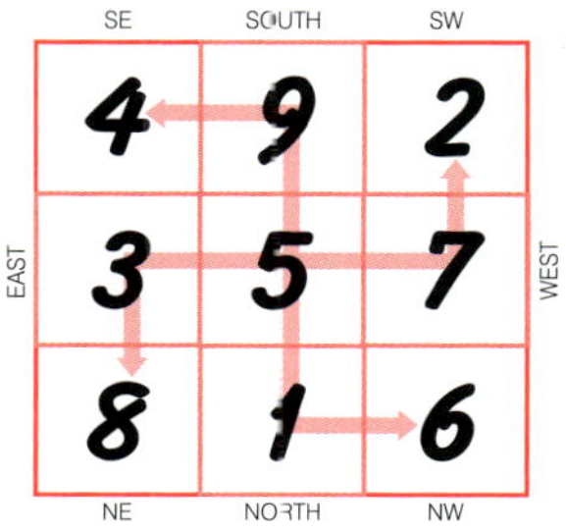

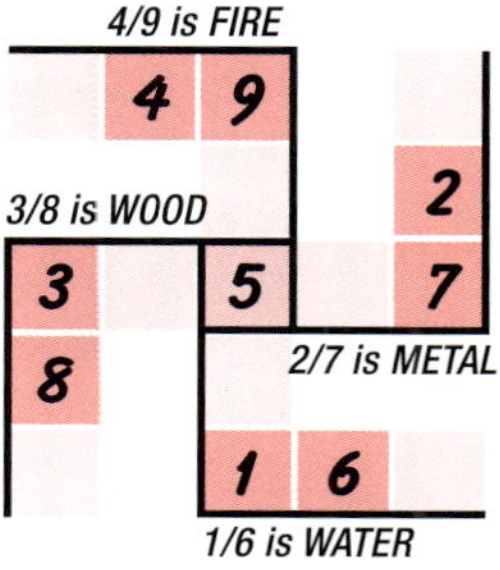

The illustration shown here summarizes the evolution of the **Lo Shu numbers** (see the square of numbers on the left) into the **Ho Tu combinations** that is presented in the diagram on the right. Note that the number 5 is in the center of the Lo Shu and the remaining numbers then create four pairs of numbers that pivot around the central number of 5.

BUDDHIST SWASTIKA

Left Turning

Straight Cross

Protection Amulet

Not to be confused with the...

NAZI SWASTIKA

Right Turning

Diagonal Cross

Power Symbol

The Ho Tu combination reflects the "movement" of the numbers going round the number 5 in an anticlockwise, or *yin* manner, in the process creating a left-turning swastika. This swastika itself is regarded as a sacred symbol, powerful and protective. It has been adopted by Buddhists who wear it as a pendant as an amulet.

This swastika is not to be confused with the Nazi swastika used by Hitler, which was right turning and the cross is a diagonal cross.

The feng shui swastika however is made up of one vertical and one horizontal line and the arms are left-turning. While the right-turning swastika brings power and a heartless attitude, the left-turning swastika brings protection and encourages a kind heart.

More significantly from a feng shui perspective is that underlying the movement of the left-turning swastika is the creation of the four sets of numbers 1 and 6, 2 and 7, 3 and 8, and 4 and 9, collectively referred to as the Ho Tu set of number combinations.

Each Ho Tu combination stands for an element, which when activated, causes four kinds of great good fortune to manifest in the sector where the Ho Tu occurs in any given year.

HO TU COMBINATIONS OF 2014

benefitting the HORSE, the ROOSTER, the RAT, the TIGER and the OX

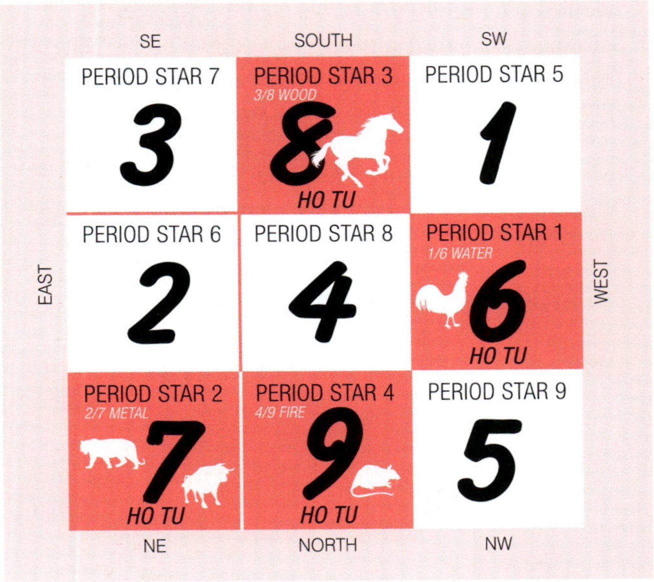

The Ho Tu combinations appear in the South, West, North and NE this year when the annual numbers combine with the period stars to give the combinations of 1/6, 2/7, 3/8 and 4/9.

The Flying Star chart of 2014 contains all four sets of Ho Tu. Here the combinations are made up of the Period of 8 numbers combining with the 2014 annual numbers. The combinations are therefore very strong. When the strength of the Ho Tu is **waxing** in sectors where the combination occurs, the Ho Tu brings amazing good fortune. Here, the word waxing is like the waxing moon – gaining brightness and brilliance. It is better than if the Ho Tu were at its peak!

The five animal signs that benefit directly from the Ho Tu combinations of 2014 are the **Tiger, Ox, Rat, Horse** and **Rooster.**

You the Rooster can also ally yourself with the Ox (your astrological ally) to borrow the energies of the **waxing Ho Tu of 2/7**, which brings the **luck of big money.** Because the Ox is closely allied with the Rooster, you will find that by simply bringing in an auspicious image of a Ox into your home direction and also into the home direction of the Ox itself, you can activate the Ho Tu of 2/7 to your benefit, especially if you also hang the **metallic windchime** that brings wealth luck. This brings the element of Metal, which energizes the Ho Tu of 2/7.

While the animal signs in the other directions benefitting from a Ho Tu may not have a special relationship with the Rooster, nevertheless, their occurrence this year holds out the promise of specific kinds of luck being available, and you need only to activate the energy of the space they have flown to in order to benefit directly or indirectly from the kind of luck they bring.

Note that if your house faces any of the four locations with the Ho Tu, you can also benefit from the combination, irrespective of your animal sign.

For instance, if your house sits Northeast or if the bedroom or your main door is located in the NE, you can directly tap into the Ho Tu of the NE and benefit from it. This is the 2/7 combination, which is described as being in the "waxing cycle in the Northeast". So it is a powerful Ho Tu that brings Big Money Luck and financial stability to whoever occupies the Northeast.

This 2/7 Ho Tu has the Metal element as its intrinsic nature. It can thus be energized by enhancing Metal and by creating the sounds of Metal in the Northeast. Hanging metallic windchimes will activate the Ho Tu here. Painting the main door a bright white colour or in a metallic shade of earth colour is also beneficial.

The power of 2/7 is enhanced during the **month of February** when the year starts. This is because in February 2014, the number 2 monthly star flies to the Northeast. This creates a **double Ho Tu** for the Northeast sector.

This pattern of number combination occurs again in the **month of November 2014** so that is once again the month when the good fortune brought by the Ho Tu occurs again. It is necessary to be physically in the North for the full force of the Ho Tu to benefit you!

North-South Axis House Exceptionally Lucky in 2014

In 2014 it is exceptionally lucky for everyone who belongs to the East group, and in particular for the **45 year old Earth Rooster male** if you are living in a house oriented to the North/South axis direction.

This is because for you the North brings the luck of *sheng chi* i.e. success and the South brings the luck of *tien yi* or good health.

We are referring to houses that face either North or South. The North/South axis means you will be facing one direction and sitting in the other direction.

When both the directions – facing and sitting – have the auspicious Ho Tu combination, **as is the case in 2014**, residents in such homes benefit from **exceptional good fortune** related to the attributes of the combination. Thus note that:

- **North** has the 4/9 Ho Tu, which brings commercial and business success.
- **South** has the 3/8 Ho Tu, which brings success in politics.

Together, the two Ho Tu combinations bring power and wealth to any home that is aligned in a North-South orientation. We have seen that Fire energy stimulates the 4/9 in the North. To stimulate the 3/8 in the South, what is needed is Wood energy, hence placing **strong growing plants** in your South sector either at the front or back of your house would bring residents a year of fast growth and enviable success.

Rooster Men & Women Enjoying the Luck of Northeast/Southwest Homes

For all Rooster women and for men who belong to the WEST group, living in a SW/NE axis direction house is very beneficial, especially during this current period of 8 when both directions Southwest and Northeast bring you good fortune. This phenomenon benefits women Roosters more than the men, because all Rooster women have either Southwest or Northeast as their *sheng chi* direction.

In fact, anyone at all will benefit from living in such houses during the current period of 8 which lasts until 2024. East group people will also benefit from these directions. This is because houses that either face Northeast or Southwest enjoy very special feng shui alignments that bring success and great abundance, **especially when water is placed at the front of the house** to signify enhancing growth chi.

Note that both the Southwest and Northeast are WEST directions, so anyone belonging to the WEST group is sure to benefit from houses that have this alignment. Note also that these two directions are beneficial for you through the entire period of 8 as Northeast is the *direct spirit* of period 8 and Southwest is the *indirect spirit* of period 8.

FENG SHUI ENHANCER: Activate the **Northeast** with the **image of a mountain** (three mountain peaks signify **excellent career luck** for descendants) to bring health and relationship luck, and activate the **Southwest** with a **water feature** to bring **wealth luck.**

Commercial Success Ho Tu for the North

The auspicious indication for the North is the occurrence of the Ho Tu combination of 4/9, which brings the luck of commercial and business success. This luck is in its waxing cycle here and it directly benefits everyone whose bedroom or doors are located in the North.

For the Rooster, while North may not be your home location, but if the North is one of your lucky directions, as it is for some of you male Roosters, you can energize the North sector to benefit you. All you need to do is simply to face North; next place a **water feature** in the North corner of your home.

Activating the North in your home can enhance your commercial success luck. Those in business will be pleased at the way profits and sales can increase when you activate the North location with a powerful water feature.

HIGH POTENCY ENHANCERS FOR 2014 (MUST-HAVES)

1. ENHANCING BRASS MIRRORS

Perfect for energizing the HO TU combinations

The big news for 2014 has to be the occurrence of **all four combinations of the Ho Tu.** This is something which everyone can and should take fullest advantage of, and one of the easiest ways to activate flying star combinations of numbers is to use **brass mirrors** that are suitably embellished with the correct symbols.

On one side should be the polished mirror surface that can reflect in the luck energy generated by the Ho Tu. In addition, it is important to have the sun and moon symbols, which reflect the waxing energy that brings good fortune, as well as an image of the **Dragon Horse**, which originally brought the Ho Tu numbers to mankind.

On the other side are the numbers and symbols that reflect the element and type of luck associated. During the *Tang Dynasty*, many different mirrors were designed for the Emperor, his court officials and their families. These often reflected the auspicious symbols they believed would activate the different kinds of good fortune desired.

In 2014, the **mirrors** you can use to activate the four Ho Tu combinations are as follows:

- **The 1/6 in the WEST sector**, which is of the Water element. This mirror has the image of the Rooster, a pattern signifying water as well as symbols of learning such as books, scrolls and brushes to signify scholastic luck. You who belong to the Rooster sign should definitely use this mirror to activate the luck of wisdom arising for you through the year. This enhances the depth of your knowledge and will improve your decisions.

The numbers 1 and 6 are represented by one book and 6 brushes. It brings wisdom to older Roosters, but this mirror can also bring excellent education luck for all school or College-going children when they place it in the West corner of their study desk and then have a **Yin Water** glass container with six black stones inside next to it.

- **The 2/7 in the NORTHEAST sector,** which is of the Metal element. This mirror has the two animal signs of the NE, the Tiger and the Ox, as well as images of gold bars and ingots to signify money as well as a stack of dollar notes. The luck of this Ho Tu combination is **the luck of big money**. It is in the waxing cycle and is strong in 2014.

If you can also hang a **brass windchime** above this enhancer mirror, it would strengthen the effect quite substantially.

- **The 3/8 in the SOUTH sector,** which is of the Wood element. This mirror has the image of the victory Horse, a pattern signifying wood ie a plant or a tree as well as the symbol of authority and power which is the Ru Yi. This combination of the Ho Tu brings **excellent luck in politics.** Energizing the sector with a mirror as described will activate for victory in elections when placed in the South corner of your desk. This combination occurring in the South is in its waxing cycle, so it is strong.

- **The 4/9 in the NORTH sector,** which is of the Fire element. This mirror has the image of the Rat in its form as a mongoose bringing pearls and jewels. This Ho Tu brings **business success and good profits.** The mirror should thus have all the symbols of asset wealth as well as income wealth. Images of a building, a ship, a lorry and a plane (4 wealth assets) and of nine ingots and gold bars are excellent symbols that reflect the combination. Place this mirror in the North corner of your desk. This combination is also in its waxing cycle.

for more on all the recommended
feng shui cures, remedies & enhancers for

2014

please log on to

www.fsmegamall.com/2014